Community Participation,
Social Development and the State

Community Participation, Social Development and the State

James Midgley
With
Anthony Hall, Margaret Hardiman and Dhanpaul Narine

Methuen
London and New York

First published in 1986 by
Methuen & Co. Ltd
11 New Fetter Lane, London EC4P 4EE

Published in the USA by
Methuen & Co.
in association with Methuen, Inc.
29 West 35th Street, New York, NY 10001

© 1986 James Midgley

Typeset by Folio Photosetting, Bristol
Printed in Great Britain by
Richard Clay (The Chaucer Press) Ltd,
Bungay, Suffolk

British Library Cataloguing in Publication Data
Midgley, James
    Community participation, social
    development and the state.
    1. Community development — Developing countries
    I. Title
    307'.14'091724   HN981.C6

    ISBN 0–416–39820–0
    ISBN 0–416–39830–8 Pbk

Library of Congress Cataloging in Publication Data
Midgley, James.
        Community participation, social development, and
the state.

        Bibliography: p.
        Includes index.
        1. Community development — developing countries —
Citizen participation. 2. Developing countries —
social policy — Citizen participation.   I. Title.
HN981.C6M52   1986   307.1'4'091724   86–5236
ISBN 0–416–39820–0
ISBN 0–416–39830–8 (pbk.)

Contents

Preface

Community participation is a new catchword in development studies and particularly in the field of social development. Popularized by the United Nations and other official bodies, it now permeates the literature on the subject. Having replaced earlier versions of formalized community development, the notion of community participation is being applied in health, education, housing, social work and urban and rural development in both non-governmental and statutory social development programmes.

However, contemporary writings on community participation are coloured with lofty sentiments and the difficulties of achieving effective community participation are not always recognized. Numerous controversies attending the idea of community participation are also neglected. Above all, the literature on the subject has not dealt adequately with the issue of the role of the state in community participation. Since the state now dominates the lives and affairs of its citizens to an extent previously unknown, community participation advocates cannot ignore the activities of the state in social development. It is naive to argue that state involvement in social development is superfluous and that local communities in the Third World can solve the serious problems of poverty and deprivation wholly through their own efforts. But it is equally naive to assume that a cosy relationship between the centralized, bureaucratic state and the local community will emerge and that political élites, professionals and administrators will readily agree to the devolution of their authority to ordinary people. While community participation is a desirable goal, the extensive involvement of the state in social development complicates the issue and requires further analysis.

This book seeks to examine the complex and controversial issue of the state and community involvement in social development in the Third World. The social development field presents useful opportunities for analysis since it is here that state involvement has expanded rapidly in the post-war decades. It is in the field of social development also that the notion of community participation is being most vigorously applied today. By examining the application of community participation ideas to different social development sectors, this book seeks to discover whether state and community involvement can be harmonized or whether the two approaches are antithetical. Hopefully, its conclusions will illuminate a complex issue and have relevance for development studies as a whole. Since the issue of community participation in the Third World has global significance, it is hoped that its conclusions will also be of interest to those in the industrial countries who are engaged in community work.

Because the personal attitudes and beliefs of social scientists inevitably affect the way they perceive reality and present their arguments, it is desirable at the outset that the views of the authors of this book be made clear. As teachers and former teachers on the social planning courses at the London School of Economics, they are all engaged in the promotion of a statist approach to social development which advocates centralized planning and direct government intervention in social welfare. Nevertheless, they are critical of the excessive bureaucratization and professionalization of state social services and believe that community participation ideals need to be promoted much more vigorously and effectively. It is this belief that has led them to examine the issue of state and community involvement in social development in a spirit of genuine enquiry.

The contributors to this volume have been asked to examine the issues independently and to reach their own conclusions about the relationship between the state and the community in social development. Although their interpretations do not diverge significantly, they nevertheless provide different insights into this question. They reveal also that community participation is not a simple matter of faith but a complex issue involving different ideological beliefs, political forces, administrative arrangements and varying perceptions of what is possible.

In writing this book, we have received much encouragement and assistance from Mary Ann Kernan of Methuen and we are grateful for her support. Gay Grant gave invaluable secretarial help which we acknowledge with gratitude. We have benefited from the views and constructive comments of Richard Estes, Gavin Kitching and

Brij Mohan; they have helped us to refine our ideas and present our arguments more clearly and cogently.

James Midgley
Anthony Hall
Margaret Hardiman
Dhanpaul Narine

Introduction: social development, the state and participation

JAMES MIDGLEY

Since the Second World War, the so-called developing societies have experienced dramatic and some would say revolutionary changes. Just a generation ago, most of these societies were under European imperial domination and subject to the absolute authority of colonial administration. Most were economically backward and wholly dependent on their imperial rulers for access to world markets, and usually their natural resources were entirely owned by metropolitan enterprises. Social conditions were appalling. Life expectancy was low, few people were literate and many were debilitated by endemic diseases.

The emancipation of the colonized societies has been accompanied by significant changes in their political, economic and social conditions. Nationalist and socialist movements which struggled for independence have taken power in the great majority of these nations. Many developing countries have experienced considerable economic progress and although few would claim that these countries have been freed from world dependency relationships, they have experienced real economic growth and unprecedented industrial development; a good number have gained greater control over their natural resources. There have also been significant gains in life expectancy and literacy in many developing countries; educational standards have improved considerably and much has been done to bring communicable diseases under control.

But while undoubted progress has been made, there is little scope for complacency. Economic growth in many developing countries has stagnated in recent years because of the world recession and the adoption of monetarist policies in the industrial countries. In a number of Third World nations, these problems have been exacerbated by political indifference, corruption and poor economic management. In the political sphere, human rights and freedoms have often been suppressed by dictatorship. The power of military élites, who often rule Third World countries directly, has adversely affected economic performance through the continued diversion of scarce domestic resources for security purposes. While significant, the social welfare gains of the last forty years are sullied by the persistence of mass poverty especially in South Asia and Sub-Saharan Africa where hundreds of millions of people live in subsistence conditions and are vulnerable to the vagaries of climate and natural disasters. Social inequalities remain marked and, in spite of progress in health and education, differential access to the social services has compounded an uneven process of social development which has characterized many developing nations.

The problems as well as the achievements of social development have been subjected to a good deal of academic scrutiny in recent times. This is due in part to a greater awareness of the continued deprivations of millions of people in the Third World and of the failure of conventional economic growth strategies to raise the levels of living of the masses. Development studies which was almost exclusively concerned with economic issues is now paying far more attention to the social dimensions of development. The contribution of sociologists, anthropologists and social policy analysts has also increased to balance the domination of Third World studies by economists. However, conceptions of social development and prescriptions for its promotion are poorly formulated and remain controversial.

Social development

Many definitions of social development are pervaded by an idealized rhetoric which often employs eloquent superlatives to describe its methods and goals. Social development is said to result in the fulfilment of people's aspirations for personal achievement and happiness, to promote a proper adjustment between individuals and their communities, to foster freedom and security and to engender a sense of belonging and social purpose. Idealized notions of participation also characterize the literature on the subject. Participation is not only one of the goals of social development but an integral part of the social development process. It is argued that social development is facilitated if people participate fully in making decisions that affect their welfare and in implementing these decisions. The mobilization of citizens in this way not only fosters improvements in social conditions but strengthens human and community bonds. Participation creates a sense of community which gives meaning to human existence and fosters social integration.

Although it might seem uncharitable to criticize these sentiments, many writers are excessively idealistic when describing the features of social development. In particular, many accounts lack specificity about practical programmes and objectives. Reference is seldom made to the planning and administrative procedures which governments employ to foster social development or to its material objectives which realize improvements in income, health, education and housing.

Some writers who have considered the practical aspects of social development have taken the view that programmes of this kind are the responsibility of public administrators, planners and economists. They claim that the social development process is concerned with non-material aspects seeking instead to strengthen community ties, foster co-operative endeavour and build institutions for social progress. It is for this reason that so little social development literature deals with the programmatic aspects of providing health, education, housing and other social services. Other writers have argued that material improvements are of limited value if people do not transcend the apathy of traditional culture and remain chained to an archaic system of superstitious and oppressive beliefs. Others have claimed that improvements in levels of living and access to social services are of little significance in societies where individual freedoms are suppressed and where individuality is subjugated to the power of the state and the bureaucratization of social life. It is only when they are liberated from these oppressive forces that human beings are able fully to utilise and enjoy the benefits of material progress.

While the significance of the ideational dimension of social development must be recognized, the current emphasis placed on abstract ideals by many social development writers needs to be put into perspective and linked with a very real need for the provision of social services which bring tangible benefits to ordinary people. In the real world, where even improvements of this kind are realized with difficulty, the prospects of perfecting human nature and creating a Utopia through social developments must be remote. It is surely more realistic to work for the achievement of attainable material goals than to hope eternally for the apotheosis of the human condition.

It is for this reason that the definition of social development used in this book is imbued with notions of material welfare and the delivery of tangible services, particularly in the fields of health, education, urban and rural development and social work services. But while little emphasis will be given to the intangible goals of social development, the cultural, political and ideological aspects of this process will feature prominently in the discussion since they are fundamental to a proper consideration of the notion of community participation in social welfare. It is meaningless to talk about community involvement in social development without examining its social and political implications.

Indeed, as will be shown, the notion of community participation is deeply ideological in that it reflects beliefs derived from social and political theories about how societies should be organized. Central to its rationale is a reaction against the centralization, bureaucratization, rigidity and remoteness of the state. The ideology of community participation is sustained by the belief that the power of the state has extended too far, diminishing the freedoms of ordinary people and their rights to control their own affairs.

The state

The exercise of political authority in modern societies is institutionalized in the processes and structures of the state. It is comprised of various organizational entities as well as a 'culture' of established traditions and formal procedures. The state's formal organizational structure comprises the various agencies or branches of government: these are conventionally classified as the executive, legislature, administration or civil service, judiciary, police and military. A distinction is commonly made between the state and the government. The government is said to consist of those agencies that make laws and carry them out. The notion of the state is broader referring to the other agencies as well as the culture of the state which transcends the actions of particular governments. However, this distinction is not always recognized and often the two terms are used interchangeably.

In recent times, there has been a tendency to reify the concept of the state and to invest it with characteristics that supersede the capacities of individuals to determine its actions. While it is true that the concentration of power in the state and the perpetuation of its conventions does give it a sociologistic quality, the state nevertheless remains a human community subject to human control and influence from both within and beyond its formal organizational structures.

The state is distinguished in its use of power from other groups, classes and associations by its claim to legitimacy in the exercise of coercion. It is this element of institutionalized authority in the enforcement of its decisions and control of citizens that characterizes state power. But while the state is equipped to employ coercion in the enforcement of law, it has other means of achieving political ends. These include a range of administrative procedures, the use of the instruments of mass communication and numerous techniques of bargaining and manipulation. But ultimately, the exercise of state power depends on legitimacy. Many political theorists have argued that the state cannot rely exclusively on coercion to implement its will. If it is to wield power efficiently and effectively, it must act in ways that are congruent with the interests and sentiments of a substantial section of the population and, in this way, sustain their support. Although the need for legitimacy is universal in that all governments must justify their monopoly of power, they seek legitimacy in different ways. In the past, legitimacy was often obtained through the identification of political power with divine authority. Today, it is more likely to arise from a congruence of ethnic or cultural identity or the appeal of nationalism, socialism or populism. Of course, legitimacy may be achieved through the cultural institutionalization of beliefs about the role of the state: the state may monopolize authority because people believe that it promotes their interests, safeguards revolutionary achievements or is subject to the sovereign will of the electorate.

Social scientists have formulated a variety of theoretical explanations of the role and functions of the state in modern societies. These may be loosely categorized into theories that stress the positive and benevolent qualities of the state and those that regard it as domineering, manipulative and sectional. While the former explanations emphasize consensus, the latter stress conflict.

Consensus accounts of the state include classical liberal democratic theory which regards the state as being subservient to the general will of the electorate. Liberals believe that the state represents the sum of the interests of its constituents: through popular elections, citizens express their aspirations granting power to elected representatives to act in their best interests. Modern functionalism offers a similar interpretation, regarding the exercise of power by the state as being essential for the maintenance of the social system and the realization of its social goals. In functionalist theory, therefore, the state embodies the interests of society as a whole. While within the same tradition, pluralism provides a somewhat different and more sophisticated interpretation. Rather than representing collective interests, pluralist theory claims that the state mediates between sectional interests compromising between the demands of various associations and classes. The theory posits that power in society is dispersed between different interest groups which compete with each other in an open political system. Although elections may further the interests of certain parties, the state remains subject to a variety of external pressures which prevent partisan interests from dominating the political process.

Very different explanations of the state are offered by theories that emphasize conflict and domination in politics. Marx's comment that the state is but a committee for managing the common affairs of the whole bourgeoisie continues to inspire contemporary Marxian interpretations. Although some neo-Marxists recognize that state–economy and state–society relationships are much more complicated than classical Marxism suggests, all agree that the state in capitalist societies is primarily concerned with accumulation. However, with the overthrow of capitalism, state power will be seized by proletarians who will govern in the interests of the proletariat. Eventually, with the advent of communism, the state will wither away. Élite theories of the state emerged partly as a reaction to the utopian elements in Marxian political thought. These theories reject the idea that the state will ever wither away and suggest instead that the domination of political life by oligarchy is both ubiquitous and inevitable. The overthrow of any élite merely results in its replacement by another élite. In its classical form, the theory holds that élites monopolize power because of the passivity and malleability of the masses and the superior intellect, organizational abilities and cunning of political entrepreneurs. In more recent versions of the theory, the power of élites is said to derive from their occupation of pivotal positions in society both within and outside the state. Entry to these positions is less dependent on personal qualities than access to élitist education or the membership of privileged groups. Together élites in various key positions in society form a coalition of interests subjugating the rest of society. The notion of coalition also characterizes the corporatist theory of the state. Recognizing the existence of large and powerful corporate groups in modern societies, the theory holds that the state seeks to articulate their influence. Although the theory recognizes the dispersal of power, it is not conceptualized in the fluid terms of pluralism but seen rather as flowing through a stable set of compromising relationships between power structures. Also, the state acts autonomously seeking to further its own interests. In the corporate society, the state manipulates, co-opts and compromises sectional interests, seeking to subordinate them to its own.

Since most of these theories appear to contain at least some valid observations and to fit the realities of at least some societies in the modern world it is very difficult to choose between them. However, most political scientists today recognize the centrality of the state in society: the state not only dominates power relationships but increasingly controls economic and social life. This expansion has been marked by the advent of state socialism in the communist countries of Eastern Europe, the rise of state welfarism in the liberal democracies and the creation of centralized political institutions in the former colonies of the European empires which have replaced older, traditional forms of authority. Everywhere public expenditures as well as bureaucratic centralization have increased and state regulation of many human activities has grown enormously.

The extension of state involvement in social development has also been rapid. State education, health, housing, social security and similar services have expanded considerably in many societies during this century and, in many, public revenue allocations to the social services have also increased. But while these developments have brought undoubted benefits to large numbers of people, there has been a growing criticism of state responsibility for welfare. Opposition has come from various quarters and varies in its intensity. The radical right has attacked the idea of state welfarism arguing that it fosters dependency and is inimical to economic growth. The Marxian left has claimed that the welfare state is a mechanism for the suppression of proletarian aspirations and the furtherance of capitalism. But it is the criticisms of the proponents of community participation that are of primary concern in this book and that require further elaboration.

Participation

Proponents of participation are critical of state social provisions arguing that they are centralized, bureaucratically administered, governed by impersonal regulations and routines and unresponsive to the problems and needs of individuals. Participation not only humanizes the bureaucracy, but strengthens the capacities of individuals and communities to mobilize and help themselves. In this way, dependence on the state is minimized and ordinary people rediscover their potential for co-operation and mutual endeavour.

While the advocates of participation in social development are undoubtedly correct in identifying the problems of statism, it has been argued that they exaggerate the problems of state welfare. Many are committed to humanistic and egalitarian ideals and should welcome an increase in collective responsibility for social development. Also, it has been argued that most people do in fact take part in community affairs and the development of their societies. Through a complex network of political, economic and other mechanisms they contribute, as citizens, to the promotion of social development ideals and the financing and implementation of programmes. Although many community participation advocates accept that people are involved in social life and that they do, therefore, participate to some extent in the affairs of the community, they believe that conventional participatory networks are inadequate. Specifically, they are concerned about two matters: the first involves the idea of real and direct involvement while the second focuses on the notion of community.

Introduction: social development, the state and participation

Proponents of community participation argue that conventional opportunities for participation in social development offer a limited scope for involvement. In liberal democracies, electors may exert some influence over the political process but this is minimal. In autocratic systems, opportunities for participation are even more curtailed and find expression largely through membership of the ruling party or otherwise of privileged classes or groups. Furthermore, they argue that the increasing centralization of the state in all societies has diminished the capacity of ordinary people to influence decisions and to contribute meaningfully to social development. They are not only politically passive but becoming increasingly dependent on state welfare. Often participation in social development results in little more than the utilization of local labour in the construction of projects. Formal opportunities for representation in the social services such as advisory bodies or official committees of local people are not regarded as particularly effective and are often thought to be manipulated by politicians and bureaucrats. To be effective, participation must be direct and give ultimate control to local communities so that they can themselves decide their own affairs.

Its advocates argue that real and direct participation in social development is needed for both instrumental and developmental reasons. Community participation serves immediate instrumental goals such as the identification of felt needs as well as the mobilization of local resources. But it also promotes broader social development ideals: by participating fully in decision-making for social development, ordinary people experience fulfilment which contributes to a heightened sense of community and a strengthening of community bonds.

The notion of community is equally important in the criticisms which have been made of state social development programmes. It is argued that representation through conventional procedures is invariably sectional so that the interests and aspirations of the whole community are seldom taken into account in the formulation and implementation of policies. Although the poorest groups are in the majority, they are the least influential and seldom able to express their views. Their powerlessness is often conveniently interpreted as passivity and indifference but the real problem is the lack of opportunity for their direct involvement. Also, state social development programmes tend to favour élite groups. Since politicians and bureaucrats are unresponsive to the needs of the disadvantaged, differential access to welfare is a real problem in many societies. To ensure that the whole community participates in decision-making for social development and shares its benefits equitably, the involvement of the disadvantaged must be actively encouraged.

The proponents of community participation are concerned then with highly specific issues. Participation requires the direct, face-to-face involvement of citizens in social development and ultimate control over decisions that affect their own welfare. Since participation must involve the whole community, the disadvantaged must be empowered to take an active part in the political process. Further propositions flow from these basic premises. In order to mobilize the deprived, external agents generally known as community workers are involved. Also, since participation must take place on a direct interpersonal basis, the unit for participation and the primary forum for the expression of views, must be the small local community.

Although the idea of community participation is exceedingly popular in development circles today, it raises difficult issues. As was suggested in the preface to this book, one of these is whether state provisions in the field of social development can be effectively harmonized with community participation ideals. Although neglected, it is an important question which this book hopes to examine in more detail.

The scope of this book

This book is specifically concerned with the issue of community participation and the state in social development in the Third World. Curiously, much of the literature on community participation has ignored the fact that the state is the major provider of social development services today and has instead treated the state as a remote, ineffective and unresponsive agent, or otherwise as being manipulative and supportive of the interests of landlords, rich farmers, businessmen and other exploiting élites. The question of state and community involvement requires proper examination. Can a balance between state and community provisions be found and, if so, is it feasible to link state and community activities in a workable relationship? To what extent can the state devolve power to local decision-making institutions and underwrite their choices financially without sacrificing its auditing role and the need to balance local, regional and national priorities? To what extent can local people co-operate with the state and take a wider view of development issues which transcends their immediate interests? Few proponents of community participation have dealt adequately with these questions and have tended instead to separate state and community elements in their writings. The few Marxian commentators who have explored this question have generally concluded that a formalization of state and community relationships in social development results inevitably in the neutralization of community initiative and the co-option of participants. Paradoxically then, instead of increasing participation, opportunities for the expression of local interests decrease it. Given the centrality of state institutions in contemporary societies, this is a depressing conclusion which requires further discussion.

The issue of state provision and community participation in social development is examined in Part II of this book. Each of its chapters, which deal with the major social services, considers the nature and extent of social need, reviews the efforts of the state to deal with it and examines the features and problems of state provision. The community participation alternative is then discussed with reference to selected case studies which highlight the feasibility and difficulties of this approach. A brief final chapter in Part III draws this material together and attempts to reach some conclusions on the question of state and community involvement in social development. In addition to its central theme, the book reviews definitions of participation and attempts to explore some of the issues attending this idea. Part I traces the historical emergence of community participation theory and practice and the various movements, ideologies and other sources of inspiration that preceded and influenced the formalization of this approach. It discusses the nature of participatory activities, examining the various images and concepts that the proponents of community participation evoke in their writings on the subject. Attention is also given to the criticisms which have been made of community participation. It will be shown that in spite of its popularity, the present-day community participation movement is faced with more complex issues and controversies than its powerful rhetoric would suggest.

PART I

1

Community participation: history, concepts and controversies

JAMES MIDGLEY

While the idea of participation is an ancient one finding expression in the cultural traditions and practices of small preliterate societies and the writings of ancient sages and philosphers, contemporary notions of community participation, as described in the introduction of this book, are of comparatively recent origin. The idea that the poor and oppressed should be mobilized by external agents and encouraged to participate in decision-making for social development at the local level has been formalized and popularized only during the last ten or fifteen years. Nevertheless, present-day conceptions of community participation have many historical antecedents and draw on a complex and varied tradition of intellectual thought.

It is worth emphasizing at the outset that current notions of community participation form part of a wider debate about popular participation in Third World development. The United Nations has been at the forefront of these discussions and together with interested academics its officials have produced a substantial literature on the subject. They have argued that a concerted effort be made to establish and strengthen institutions for the mobilization of popular participation in developing countries. By involving people actively in the development process, attempts to promote economic and social progress are accelerated. At the same time, popular participation ensures that the benefits of development are equitably distributed. To further popular participation, proposals have been made for the decentralization of government, the redistribution of income and wealth, improved access to education and other social services and the creation of new employment opportunities. While the idea of community participation in social development emerged as a part of the broader popular participation debate, it is more specific in its focus on deprived and disadvantaged groups in small communities and with the mechanisms of direct involvement in decision-making. Its leading proponents are also to be found in the international agencies: in addition to the United Nations, community participation ideals have been enthusiastically endorsed by officials at the World Health Organization and at UNICEF. They have also been championed by non-governmental development organizations and by academics at universities in both the developing and industrial countries.

This chapter will briefly review the historical emergence of community participation and, in somewhat more detail, examine its conceptual content. Attention will also be given to the controversies that attend the idea of community participation. One of these, which is the primary focus of this book, is the role of the state in the promotion of community participation. Although this controversy will be considered in more detail in the remaining chapters, a framework for examining the issue of state involvement in community participation will be provided here.

The historical antecedents of community participation

Although it is often assumed that community participation is a new idea in development studies, current community participation concepts are based on a rich legacy of ideas and practical agendas which have helped to facilitate the formulation of present-day proposals for the involvement of local people in social development. It is, of course, impossible to review these antecedents here in any detail but some of the more important influences on contemporary community participation theory and practice require elaboration. Among these are western ideologies and political theories, the Third World community development movement of the 1950s and 1960s and finally western social work and community radicalism; each requires a brief discussion.

Community participation: history, concepts and controversies

The legacy of western ideology

Of the various historical influences on the development of current community participation principles, the debt to western democratic theory would seem to be the most obvious. By arguing that ordinary citizens have a right to share in decision-making, proponents of community participation reveal the inspiration of democratic ideals. However, this inspiration is not based on classical notions of representative democracy (Schumpeter, 1942; Dahl, 1956; Lucas, 1976; Pennock, 1979) but rather on a modern variant of liberal democratic theory known as neighbourhood democracy (Dahl and Tufts, 1973). Indeed, many proponents of community participation are sceptical of representative democracy and its possibility of providing meaningful opportunities for the involvement of the masses in the political affairs of developing countries. Drawing on the theory of neighbourhood democracy, they advocate the creation of small scale institutions for the realization of political aspirations in the villages and urban neighbourhoods of the Third World.

The views of the proponents of community participation are also infused with populist notions which, Wiles (1969, p. 166) pointed out, are characterized by the belief that 'virtue resides in the simple people who are in the overwhelming majority and in their collective traditions'. There are many definitions of populism but as Stewart (1969) observed, common to all of them is the idea that ordinary folk are badly done by. They may be perceived to be the victims of economic disruption or thought to suffer from the arrogance of an inflexible bureaucracy or it may be believed that they are neglected by an indifferent establishment. In these circumstances, populist movements often arise to champion the cause of the masses and to rally their support.

Populism has considerable influence in development studies and also in the developing countries where it has been embraced by political leaders, intellectuals and technocrats. Worsley (1967) pointed out that the development plans of many Third World countries are strongly populist in character placing emphasis on co-operative and communitarian forms of social and economic organization, stressing the values of self-help and self-sufficiency. The mixed economy is accepted and the proclaimed objective of the plans is to promote agriculture and improve the levels of living of the masses. Modernization of the economy through the promotion of heavy industry is regarded as inappropriate to the needs of the people. Kitching (1982) defined populism in a similar way pointing out that its major exponents in recent times have included President Nyerere, officials at the ILO concerned with the World Employment Programme, Schumacher and the Intermediate Technology Development Group and Lipton (1977).

The influence of populist ideas on the advocates of community participation has been very considerable; indeed, it may be argued that community participation principles are a primary expression of populist ideals in the Third World today. As in populism, current community participation theory suggests that ordinary people have been exploited by politicians and bureaucrats and that they have been excluded not only from political affairs but from the development process in general. Their simple way of life is threatened by the forces of modernization and rapid social change and they face increasing hardship as a result of economic and political mismanagement. By organizing local people and making them aware of their situation, community participation provides a mechanism for the mobilization of the masses and a collective means of redress.

Anarchism has also had an influence on community participation but this influence has been more subtle than that of populism. Anarchist ideas are most noticeable in the work of those writers who have taken an anti-statist attitude arguing that the formal institutions of the modern state are inimical to the emergence of spontaneous forms of social and political organization. Central to their work is the belief that authority, and particularly the institutionalization of coercive authority in the organs of the state (of whatever ideology or proclaimed intention), is a primary source of oppression. To realize both freedom and welfare, the state must be destroyed.

Of the various forms of anarchism, Kropotkin's version of anarcho-communism, with its romantic and naturalistic tendencies, is probably closest to contemporary community participation ideals. His insistence that co-operation and mutualism are natural human instincts and characteristic of primordial social organization, is frequently echoed in the literature. Many contemporary community participation advocates also share his belief that instinctive human capacities for communalism and participation will re-emerge when the corrupting influence of the state are removed. His Utopian formulae for the reorganization of society into a voluntary federation of communes run wholly on egalitarian principles is paralleled in the writings of those who urge the creation of small, self-sufficient communities which will promote social development and maximize community participation in the Third World.

The influence of community development

The community development movement of the 1950s and 1960s is another source of inspiration for contemporary community participation theory. Indeed, the two approaches have much in common. Like community participation, community development focused on small communities, seeking to establish democratic decision-making institutions at the local level. It attempted also to mobilize people to improve their social and economic circumstances through undertaking a variety of development projects (Brokensha and Hodge, 1969). But there are also clear differences. Community participation theory evolved partly in response to the criticisms which have been made of the community development movement. By reacting to its inadequacies, community participation advocates have sought to formulate a more politicized and people-centred approach which conceives of participation in a more dynamic way.

Among the first proponents of community development were missionaries and colonial officials; indeed, as Mayo (1975) pointed out, colonialism itself created the climate in which community development was to take shape. The dual mandate to civilize while exploiting, the use of forced labour under the pretext that it was an indigenous institution and the need to establish durable and responsible political structures, all facilitated the evolution of early forms of community development. In Africa, missionary effort to promote education led to the creation by the Colonial Office in London of the Advisory Committee on Native Education which produced a number of reports on colonial educational policy. The 1944 report on *Mass education in the Colonies* was particularly important for it placed emphasis on literacy training and advocated the promotion of agriculture, health and other social services through local self-help. The British government implemented many of the recommendations of the report and established community development programmes in many African countries; it also supported training and research in the field. These latter activities produced a variety of books and manuals on the subject of which those by Batten (1962, 1965) are perhaps the best known. In India, as Bhattacharyya (1970) observed, community development drew inspiration from both missionary and indigenous sources. Of the indigenous sources, the Utopian experiments of Tagore and Gandhi were particularly important; after independence when the Indian community development programme was launched, the debt to Gandhi's philosophy was obvious.

Drawing extensively on the British literature and the African and Indian experience, the United Nations and the American government contributed further to the refinement of community development ideas. Community development featured prominently in United Nations documents which were published in the 1950s and 1960s and the organization actively encouraged the promotion of these activities. The American aid programme provided liberal financial support to Third World governments establishing schemes of this kind and a number of American academics were recruited as advisers and experts. A particular motive for American financial aid was a desire to contain subversive influences. It is not surprising, as Brokensha and Hodge (1969) pointed out, that American community development expenditures were highest in countries such as Thailand and Vietnam which were considered to be most threatened by communism.

In spite of the rapid expansion of community development, disillusionment with its achievements was widespread by the 1970s. Many governments, particularly in Africa, failed to provide adequate financial support but nevertheless extolled the virtues of self-help. Community development was soon recognized by the people to amount to little more than a slogan which brought few tangible benefits. In many African countries, civil servants came to regard community development as a relatively unimportant field of public service and as Ministries of Education lost interest, community development activities were promoted on a haphazard basis by poorly funded Ministries of Social Welfare instead. Corruption, maladministration and inefficiency were rampant and it often seemed that the only beneficiaries of community development were the workers and officials who staffed the creaking community development bureaucracies. An indication of the declining fortunes of community development is revealed in the decision of the Indian government in 1978 to restructure its community development programme, renaming it the Integrated Rural Development Programme instead.

Although community development may be regarded as an immediate precursor to the community participation movement, contemporary community participation advocates have been vociferous critics of community development claiming that it failed because of its bureaucratic administration and superimposed direction. This not only stifled the innate capacities of ordinary people to determine their own destiny but perpetuated the structures of inequality and oppression both at the national and local level. They argue that an alternative grass-roots approach, which liberates the powerless and ensures their involvement in community life, is needed to promote genuine participatory development.

The contribution of western social work and community radicalism

Although social work is primarily concerned with the problems of needy individuals and their families, it has also, since its inception in the late nineteenth century, focused on communities seeking to organize and mobilize people to improve local amenities and social services. Among the first attempts to systematize community work practice and give it a theoretical base were the reports edited by Lane (1939, 1940) for the National Council on Social Work in the United States. Later publications by Ross (1955, 1958), Warren (1955), and Harper and Dunham (1959) refined these ideas and helped to establish community organization (as it became known) as an accepted method of social work. In the 1960s, community organization ideas were further developed by writers such as Morris (1964), Ecklein and Lauffer (1972) and Perlman and Gurin (1972) to incorporate notions of social planning into community organization procedures.

The development of community organization in Europe lagged behind and was largely influenced by American ideas (National Council for Social Service, 1960; Hendriks, 1964; Thomas, 1983) even though existing activities such as youth work and community planning in the new towns provided a basis for the development of local practice methods. In spite of this, American style community organization was never fully adopted and instead, a more radical style of community work took root. This approach transformed conventional methods of community work: instead of seeking to help deprived communities to improve their social and environmental circumstances, the new community work activists urged that people take direct political action to demand changes and improvements. One important source of inspiration for community work radicalism in the west was the ideas and activities of Alinsky (1946, 1971) in Chicago in the 1930s and 1940s. In the Back of the Yards campaign, Alinsky mobilized local people through existing grassroots organizations teaching them to use a variety of confrontational tactics when dealing with government organizations and commercial interests. Another was the War on Poverty in the United States which facilitated the institutionalization of radicalism in community work practice. There were similar developments in Britain in the late 1960s, when the Wilson government announced that it would establish community projects in particularly deprived inner city areas as a part of its Urban Programme. Although the projects were originally based on conventional community organization techniques, they were soon influenced by more radical community action approaches and also by Marxian ideas. The initial assumptions of the projects that poverty could be reduced by local improvements, the provision of better services and the stimulation of community interest, soon lost appeal and many workers began to see their task as one of raising the political consciousness of the poor. As Loney (1983, p. 131) observed, this reflected the influence of an increasingly popular structural approach in community work which 'focused on economic, social and political factors in seeking to account for deprivation rather than on individual, family or cultural factors'. Armed with this ideology, local project activists took control of the community development projects and tensions between them and their governmental sponsors increased.

While the American and British community action experiments resulted in the creation of few really durable projects, they infused community work with a new dynamism which institutionalized radicalism as an essential ingredient of practice. Although this radicalism has seldom been expressed in revolutionary or subversive acts, it has changed the nature of community work in the industrial countries.

It has also had considerable appeal in the Third World. Midgley (1981) noted that community action ideas have had some popularity in social work circles in developing countries and Marsden and Oakley (1982) reported that many non-governmental organizations had adopted radical community work methods. Some, such as the Community Action Movement in Maharashtra, India, adopted an explicit Marxian ideology which rejected 'welfarism' and sought instead to promote a 'political struggle based on a class analysis of Indian society and the organization of the oppressed majority' (p. 158). Although it cannot be claimed that the contemporary community participation movement in the Third World is characterized by a similar ideology, it has been much influenced by community work radicalism in the west.

The emergence of community participation

While the three historical antecedents described already provided a source of inspiration for current community participation theory, its emergence as a coherent approach to social development must be seen as a direct consequence of the United Nations' popular participation programme. Surveying the activities of the United Nations in this field, Wolfe (1982) observed that the concept of popular participation was broadly conceived; popular participation not only required the creation of opportunities for political involvement but the adoption of measures that would enable ordinary people to share fully in the development process.

The emphasis on popular participation in United Nations thinking was formalized with the publication of two major documents on the subject in the 1970s. The first, *Popular Participation in Development* which was published in 1971, reviewed the emergence of the idea with reference to community development in the Third World during the preceding twenty-five years. The second, *Popular Participation in Decision Making for Development* which was published in 1975, offered a formal definition of the concept with reference to its implementation. The publication of these documents was followed by the creation of a major research programme into popular participation by the United Nations Research Institute for Social Development (UNRISD) in Geneva. As Stiefel and Pearse (1982) reported, participation was to become one of the major themes around which the organization's activities were to develop. Further reinforcement for the idea of popular participation came from resolutions adopted at the World Conference on International Women's Year which was held in Mexico

City in 1975 (United Nations, 1976c) which observed that women had been excluded from participating both in political activities and the development process in the Third World.

Although nebulous and diffuse, the popular participation idea soon inspired more specific conceptions of community level involvement in social development. Recognizing that the notion of popular participation was very broad, the United Nations convened a meeting of experts in 1978 to consider the specific issue of community level participation (United Nations, 1981).

But a more significant contribution came from agencies such as UNICEF and the World Health Organization and especially in the adoption of the UNICEF/WHO *Declaration on Primary Health Care* at the Alma Ata Conference in 1977. The concept of community participation in health featured prominently in this document and has, as De Kadt (1982, p. 573) observed, become a 'major preoccupation in the health field'. The adoption of this declaration followed growing concern about the inappropriateness of health policies in developing countries; it emphasized the provision of basic services in local communities instead which would provide basic health care, preventive services, nutrition, maternal and child health and the utilization of simple medical technologies. Above all, it called for the mobilization of local communities to take responsibility for their own health. UNICEF and WHO were optimistic that 'health by the people' was feasible; indeed, several collections of country case studies (Djukanovics and Mach, 1975; Newell, 1975; Hetzel, 1978) gave ground for optimism demonstrating that community based primary health programmes were already functioning in a number of countries.

During the 1970s, the idea of popular participation also attracted attention from those engaged in housing and urban development research. Although proposals for aided self-help housing had been made earlier by Koenigsberger (1952) and Abrams (1964), it was largely through the work of Turner (1967, 1968) that these ideas were popularized. The initiative was taken by the World Bank which modified its housing sector lending policies to promote self-help housing in the Third World. In 1975, the Bank's *Housing: Sector Policy Paper* stated that squatter upgrading and sites and services schemes 'are primary lending instruments for more equitable urban development' (p. 45). By 1980, the Bank had loaned US 1.3 million dollars to developing countries for schemes of this kind;

forty-one projects had been established and by 1983, another ninety projects would be approved (World Bank, 1980). Through the influence of the international agencies, the governments of many developing countries have acknowledged the need for greater emphasis on community based development strategies and some have taken steps to strengthen participatory elements in their social development programmes. Of course, some governments have also established their own programmes based on indigenous populist, nationalist or traditional beliefs. Nongovernmental organizations have also been major promoters of community participation ideals. International voluntary agencies ranging from OXFAM and the World Council of Churches have been particularly enthusiastic about community participation ideas and many academics, especially in the field of development studies regard community participation as a new and viable approach to social development. Although little is known about the activities of local and national voluntary organizations in the Third World, many of them, including national charities, indigenous populist movements and village based associations have popularized the ideals of community participation. But, as will be shown, the belief in the undoubted virtue of involving people in development is not as straightforward or uncontroversial as it might at first appear.

The concept of community participation

A distinction has previously been made between the concept of popular participation and community participation. While the former is concerned with broad issues of social development and the creation of opportunities for the involvement of people in the political, economic and social life of a nation, the latter connotes the direct involvement of ordinary people in local affairs. Although popular participation and community participation may be distinguished, they are obviously interlinked. Both concepts are inspired by similar ideals and connote similar processes. Indeed, many definitions of community participation draw on United Nations resolutions which were adopted in the early 1970s. One definition of this kind was formulated by a group of experts appointed to discuss community level action in popular participation. It defined participation as:

The creation of opportunities to enable all members of a community and the larger society to actively contribute to and influence the development process and to share equitably in the fruits of development (United Nations, 1981, p. 5)

While suitable as a working definition, this formulation of the concept is typically general and obtuse and it raises many further questions. Also, it lacks specificity about the nature of the programmes required to promote participation. Clearly, much more information is needed if we are to know *who* participates, *what* participation entails and *how* it can be promoted. To obtain a better understanding of these wider issues it is necessary to transcend the formal definitions and to review the literature in a little more detail.

The image of community

Although it may appear to be self-evident that the proponents of community participation are referring to communities when discussing *who* participates, the concept of community is poorly defined in the literature even though it is central to the issue. Most authorities do not seek to define the term formally and instead use it loosely to denote a socio-spatial entity. However, the United Nations (1975a) pointed out that the notion of locality in these descriptions is ambiguous: it can refer simultaneously to neighbourhoods, villages, districts, towns and even cities. It is more useful, the organization suggested, to conceive of community participation as taking place in small communities comprised of individuals 'at the lowest level of aggregation at which people organize for common effort' (p. 31).

The notion of 'lowest level of aggregation' is implicit in the way various writers define the community: they focus on the smallest units of socio-spatial organization often evoking the idea of the village. But they seldom differentiate between different kinds of rural communities and instead two archetypal images pervade the literature: one is the traditional African village and the other is the semi-feudal Asian or Latin American peasant settlement. Almost no reference is made to communities of hunter gatherers, pastoral nomads or shifting cultivators. Urban communities do not feature prominently in the literature and generally they are discussed separately in publications dealing with urban problems (United Nations, 1976a; Hollnsteiner, 1977, 1982b). In these publications, the urban community is usually conceived of as a slum or squatter settlement.

Although definitions of community vary, most authors do relate the concept of community participation to notions of deprivation and disadvantage. The proponents of community participation are clearly not concerned with affluent apartment dwellers or wealthy suburbanites or with landowners or rich farmers or other rural élites. Although many have pointed out that the concept refers to impoverished villages or urban neighbourhoods, they fail to recognize that deprived communities are not homogeneous and that inequalities of one kind or another characterize most forms of social organization. Deprived rural communities and urban squatter settlements are comprised of the poor, the very poor and the not so poor who have differential access to resources. While some authors argue that only those sections of the village or neighbourhood that are the most disadvantaged should be mobilized for participation, others believe that the whole community should be involved. For example, Hollnsteiner (1982a, p. 39) maintained that 'people's participation refers not to everyone in an identifiable community – since local élites already have a strong voice in decision-making – but rather to the poor majority with little access to resources and power'. On the other hand, White (1982) insisted that community participation is not concerned with the mobilization of some individuals who should be regarded as the beneficiaries of participation; rather it involves the 'participation of the organized community as such' (p. 19).

The idea of participation

Although there are different views about *what* participation entails, many writers quote the United Nations Economic and Social Council resolution 1929 (LVIII) when discussing this issue. This resolution states that participation requires the voluntary and democratic involvement of people in '(a) contributing to the development effort, (b) sharing equitably in the benefits derived therefrom and (c) decision-making in respect of setting goals, formulating policies and planning and implementing economic and social development programmes'. These three elements suggest, therefore, that a community participates in social development if the poorest groups in the community have an effective role in choosing social development programmes, if they contribute together with the rest of the community in the implementation of decisions and if they derive equitable benefits from these programmes. Most authorities stress also that involvement of this kind facilitates a more generalized involvement of the poor in the life of the community so that it is able to act democratically in its dealings with the outside world.

Several writers have distinguished between authentic participation which involves all three criteria mentioned previously and pseudo-participation which limits community involvement to implementation or the ratification of decisions already taken by external bodies. White (1982) observed that the involvement of the population in implementation can hardly be considered to be community participation unless 'there is at least some degree of sharing of decisions with the community' (p. 19). Another type of pseudo-participation, Bugnicourt (1982) noted, is the typical African co-operative whose statutes, internal regulations and modes of operation have been predetermined by officials whom local people do not support.

However, the notion of authentic participation is very ambitious. Few community participation proponents recognize that there are formidable difficulties in fully involving all sections of the community in all aspects of social development and equally few consider the practical problems of advocating full autonomy over local affairs. Indeed, most definitions of community participation are distinctly Utopian in character. The United Nations Research Institute for Social Development (1980) employed a typically superlative style when describing the notion of authentic participation. This notion, it claimed, can be distinguished from pseudo-participation because it is not imposed from above but arises from the grass-roots; it focuses on distribution becoming a means of obtaining a larger share in the fruits of development and heightens the participants' awareness of their own capabilities to make choices and influence outcomes. In addition, other writers have argued that community participation strengthens interpersonal relationships, fosters self-confidence, improves material conditions and reduces feelings of powerlessness and alienation (United Nations, 1975a, 1981; Majeres, 1977; White, 1982; Hollnsteiner, 1977, 1982a).

The ambitious character of current concepts of community participation is revealed also in the prerequisites for participation which have been identified by various writers. Reports by members of UNRISD's Popular Participation Programme (Pearse and Stiefel, 1979, 1982) have consistently claimed that authentic participation requires 'profound social structural change' and a 'massive redistribution of power'. A United Nations report went further, pointing out that the involvement of the poor will not only need 'a change in domestic political institutions but a change in the international economic order' (1981, p. 9).

Another element in many definitions of participation is the emphasis placed on autonomy and self-reliance in participation. The United Nations (1981) distinguished between spontaneous, induced and coerced participation. While coerced participation was soundly condemned, and induced participation regarded as second best, spontaneous participation came closest 'to an ideal mode of participation as it reflects a voluntary and autonomous action on the part of the people to organize and deal with their problems unaided by government or other external agents' (p. 8). UNICEF's (1982) operational definition of participation also emphasizes self-reliance and autonomy. Community participation is said to be achieved when programmes which are desired and utilized by the community are effectively sustained by them after all external support has been phased out.

It is on this point that the notion of community participation as *practice* becomes relevant. Some writers believe that deprived communities cannot function autonomously without having first been made aware of their capacity for independent collective action and taught the techniques of interacting with external agencies. This, they argue, requires the assistance of skilled community workers who can mobilize support and inculcate an attitude of confidence and co-operation. Other experts take the view that poor communities have an inherent capacity for participation and that they are not only able to organize themselves but do so already. Since their views are highly relevant to a discussion of *how* community participation takes place, they require further elaboration.

The potential for community participation

Publications by the United Nations generally take the view that poor communities have little potential for participation. One report (1981) referred to the 'backward state' of rural communities pointing out that 'it is difficult to arouse the poor from their apathy and indifference to development issues' (p. 16). Another (1975a) claimed that traditional forms of participation based on institutionalized reciprocity and communal self-help were of little significance. Although people will collaborate to harvest crops, prepare for festivals and ceremonies and even contribute towards community projects, 'these efforts do not form the basis for a continued involvement in community affairs' (p. 35). In the urban areas, where poor people co-operate to establish squatter settlements and improve their environment, the United Nations (1976a) observed that these projects usually have a short life span and require external assistance if they are to survive.

Much of the earlier literature on community development was equally pessimistic about the potential for community development. Rural people were said to be bound by traditionalism and a tenacious resistance to progress which could only be overcome through the intervention of external agents. Some writers, such as Dasgupta (1968) even argued that the provision of material benefits to deprived communities is meaningless unless they are first mobilized to recognize their inner potential for dynamic growth. Surprisingly, the conscientization movement has also been paternalistic about the nature of peasant culture. But instead of attributing apathy and indifference to traditional culture, it has blamed political and structural factors; it has also claimed that external intervention is required to change the prevailing attitudes of the poor.

Other writers have a different view of deprived communities arguing that they are not as passive and disorganized as has been suggested. Hakim (1982) emphasized the ability of the poor to take positive steps to improve their circumstances. Drawing on his experience of Latin America and the Caribbean, he claimed that 'poor people know what they require to satisfy their interests, meet their needs and solve their problems' (p. 138). Although they make mistakes and are not always aware of the obstacles they face, they learn from their experiences and this strengthens their capacity for co-operative endeavours. On the basis of a study in Sierra Leone, Midgley and Hamilton (1978) concluded that rural communities are not disinterested in development: all of the villages in their sample had undertaken co-operative projects without any external assistance and although they had experienced many difficulties, they were capable of spontaneous involvement.

Although most authors take sides on this question, it is obvious that the capacity of communities to engage in participatory activities is highly variable. Communities are comprised of individuals who differ in their desires to become involved or who are constrained by various factors from participating. Also, people become involved to a lesser or greater degree at different times and in response to different issues. Sociological factors are also relevant: obviously, communities that are fragmented into different factions or divided by culture, religion or other allegiances will not co-operate as effectively as those that are cohesive and well integrated.

Promoting community participation

Many proponents of community participation are concerned with how new mechanisms for community participation, that conform to the principles described earlier, can be established. As well as being an ideal, therefore, community participation is a specific process involving the use of prescribed techniques and procedures.

A major element in most discussions on the promotion of community participation is the notion of institution building. This concept has been formulated by the international agencies to denote the creation of procedures for democratic decision-making at the local level and the involvement of people in these procedures to the extent that they regard them as the normal way of conducting community affairs. Many authorities use the term to connote the establishment of decision-making bodies that are fully representative, democratically elected and accountable. However, some writers place greater emphasis on the formalization of these procedures than others. Majeres (1977) conceived of local institutions as properly constituted authorities linked to district, regional and national decision-making bodies by legal and administrative procedures. Omer (1981) took a similar view, citing the Chinese commune and the Israeli Kibbutz as examples of ideal local level participatory institutions. Others (Hollnsteiner, 1977, 1982a; Hakim, 1982) have a preference for less structured grass-roots associations that are sustained by popular involvement and support. But whether local institutions are formally or informally organized, most writers point out that the major task for community workers is to foster their consolidation and effective functioning in the long term.

Community workers who are entrusted with the task of institutional building are also referred to in the literature as change agents, extension workers, motivators, community organizers, *animateurs* or conscientizers. These workers have been trained at universities or colleges to promote community participation ideals. They are skilled in understanding interpersonal relationships, fostering group activities and promoting community solidarity and in teaching local people to be resourceful in their dealings with the outside world. Although they are of both sexes and equally competent, it is generally accepted that women workers are most effective when working with women in the community (UNICEF, 1982).

Community workers are usually posted to local communities by a sponsoring agency which also funds them and provides other forms of support. Ideally, local communities should be encouraged to invite a community worker to live in their midst and to contribute to their maintenance. Hollnsteiner (1979) hoped that communities will do so spontaneously if they are faced with problems and have heard of what community workers can do for them. But most community workers are today sponsored by formal organizations such as the churches, voluntary agencies, ideologically motivated groups, the international agencies and, increasingly, the governments of Third World countries. Often the activities of these workers are related to a project that the sponsoring organization has established in the community.

Workers begin by taking up residence in the community and by seeking to establish informal contacts with local people. Although they will inevitably deal with traditional leaders and local élites, they are primarily concerned with the poorest groups attempting to organize them and to secure their full involvement in the institution building process. They will attach particular importance to the mobilization of women. Although women comprise approximately a half of the community, they are seldom consulted and it is for this reason that organizations such as UNICEF makes a special effort to ensure that they are actively involved in its participatory programmes. UNICEF has found that its projects have benefited from the participation of women who have a particularly useful contribution to make to social development.

A major priority is to raise the level of social and political consciousness of local people. Hollnsteiner (1982a, p. 48) observed that by conscientizing the people, community workers 'make them consciously aware of their life situation, why it is so and what alternatives they have or can create to redress its deficiencies'. Part of this process entails the use of confrontational tactics that create an awareness of problems and possibilities. Hollnsteiner (1979, p. 409) pointed out that community workers engage in 'persuading, arguing, suggesting, challenging, analysing and agitating in building people's organizations'. This is a particularly important technique for integrating the poorest and more privileged sections of the community and for fostering collective solidarity.

Mass meetings are an essential element in the promotion of community participation. These meetings permit the discussion of local issues and help to foster group solidarity. Often, role play methods are used to sensitize the people to both local and external problems. However, community workers never tell the community what to do. Their task is to foster grass-roots participation and to build local institutions that can take decisions democratically and autonomously. Community workers must, as Hollnsteiner (1979) observed, know where to draw the line between being a catalyst and a manipulator. Also, instead of seeking to impose their own ideological preferences on the community, they allow local people to form their own views and make their own decisions on these wider issues.

Leadership poses a problem for community workers. They cannot themselves act as leaders and where traditional élites are reactionary and unresponsive, they cannot develop their pro-grammes around existing leadership roles. Nor can they appoint alternative leaders since these should emerge naturally. They are, however, trained to deal with the problems of leadership and have various tactics at their disposal. They may succeed in isolating reactionary elements or persuade them to abide by the wishes of the majority. They may also be able to integrate both traditional and emergent leaders in the new decision-making bodies and in this way, build a coalition of interests that unites the different factions. However, they are wary of placing too much responsibility on individual leaders and particularly of allowing a charismatic individual to dominate. Although inspirational leadership may mobilize people and resources effectively, the emergence of strong and enduring collective institutions is retarded. Also, as Hakim (1982) noted, dependence on charismatic leaders is associated with a high rate of project failure. If these leaders lose interest or cease to function for other reasons, community participation programmes often collapse.

Many authorities have pointed out that community participation can be effectively initiated through the creation of specific projects that command popular support. Indeed, as Pearse and Stiefel (1982) pointed out, attempts to foster community participation are often linked to the introduction of particular social development projects. However, several writers have warned of an excessive reliance on projects as a basis for promoting participation. The United Nations (1975a) pointed out that the project can easily become an end in itself and that participation will decline once it is completed. There is a danger also that in the rush to construct facilities, community involvement will be overlooked and that the people's role will be relegated to implementation.

Training for participation is recommended by several authorities who argue that in addition to the efforts of community workers to train local people in participatory skills, more structured opportunities for training should be created within and outside the locality. External trainers should be brought in to hold workshops on various topics and specialist skills in a variety of social development activities should be provided. Community leaders should be sent on training courses to improve their organizational, administrative and leadership abilities and to learn the techniques of project development, implementation, monitoring and evaluation.

A major topic in the literature on community participation is the idea of decentralization. The discussion on this issue has been actively fostered by the United Nations (1975a, 1981) which has called for the establishment or strengthening of local decision-making bodies in developing countries. The tendency towards centralization, it is argued, must be resisted since ordinary people are becoming increasingly excluded from political affairs.

Decentralization requires the creation of effective and democratically elected and representative decision-making bodies with clearly defined powers to administer programmes and control revenues. Majeres (1977) has argued that the unit for decentralization should be a local development council which should be empowered to assume responsibility for the administration of local level programmes and to initiate a variety of infrastructural and social development projects of its own. As these councils become firmly established, their powers should be extended to administer a variety of additional services. They should be formally linked to higher tier authorities and serve as a channel for communicating ideas and innovations upwards. They should also, as the United Nations (1981, p. 23) suggested 'be integrated into the formal administrative and planning process'.

A major problem facing the proponents of decentralization and one of general relevance to community participation, is finance. True decentralization only occurs when local decision-making bodies have control over financial resources. Since they are usually unable to raise sufficient revenues to meet their own needs, they are dependent on external funds and thus subject to external control. Majeres (1977) has advocated that local bodies should receive direct central government support which should be allocated in terms of criteria such as population numbers and social need indicators. Their rights to budgetary support should be enshrined in law. Local bodies should also be permitted to raise their own funds and be given access to credit and the freedom to allocate resources as they see fit. However, Majeres recognized that external audit and specifications about how central government funds should be spent, will be necessary.

Since decentralization is linked to the formalization of procedures and the institutional regulation of local decision-making bodies by higher tier authorities, those who favour non-formal community organization have not said much on the subject. Although they recognize the interdependence of local communities and the wider society, they stress mass involvement, autonomy, spontaneity and informality rather than the regularization of procedures and organizational structures. They believe also that local communities should deal with external authorities from a position of strength and they are fearful that formalization will weaken the community's position. In this interpretation of community participation, emphasis is placed on conflict and confrontation rather than the routinization of dialogue and exchange. For Stiefel and Pearse (1982, p. 146) participation is an encounter between local people and the rest of society, between grass-roots interests and inflexible establishments and between villages and metropolitan interests. As they put it: 'The hitherto excluded strata confront the supporters and controllers of sets of social arrangements which determine patterns of access to resources, services, status and power, seeking a new deal'. Confrontational tactics which include protests, occupations, the constant badgering of officials and other forms of militant action, are an effective way of securing resources for deprived communities. But these techniques should not, Hollnsteiner (1979, p. 414) argued, be regarded as a form of violence but rather as a way of 'building up a dialogue between the parties where none was possible before'. They are much more effective than the formalized, institutional approach and serve also as a useful mechanism for mobilizing community solidarity.

Problems and controversies in community participation

The proponents of community participation have made a powerful and emotionally appealing case. Participation is advocated not only because it facilitates social service delivery by lowering costs and smoothing implementation but because it fosters a sense of belonging and the integration of communities: this, in turn, helps local people to contribute positively to national development. To criticize community participation ideals would, therefore, appear to be ungenerous. But however much they may sympathize with noble ideas, social scientists are professionally bound to apply their analytical skills to examine the weaknesses, inconsistencies and difficulties of any set of beliefs. However, this is not an easy task. Because the literature of community participation is permeated with moral sentiments, it is not only a question of criticizing ideals that have intrinsic appeal but of disentangling ethical issues from theoretical and practical considerations.

Several writers have commented on the lofty sentiments of the advocates of community participation. As was shown previously, the literature on the subject is characterized by heroic and millennial images. Community workers are cast as the champions of the poor who apply their skills and knowledge to unite a demoralized populace and to forge them into a self-reliant and cohesive community which will engage the forces of oppression and secure justice and improvements in welfare for all. Although there is nothing wrong with idealism, these notions are so infused with moral sentiments that conceptual clarity and rigour have been sacrificed. As De Kadt (1982, p. 174) noted, the concept of community participation 'has popularity without clarity and is subject to growing faddishness and a lot of lip service'.

The concept of the small community as a cohesive and integrated entity fighting for justice against powerful external forces is inspired by the romanticism of populist thought rather than a serious analysis of community life and its complex characteristics and dynamics. It has been argued already that even deprived communities are differentiated in terms of status, income and power. Nor is it recognized that poor people do not always behave in the nicest way towards each other. As Elliott (1975) observed, the exploiters in many poor communities are comparatively small fish who are themselves poor and exploited in turn by others. Similarly, studies of urban squatter settlements (Dwyer, 1975; Lloyd, 1979) have shown that poor squatter communities are highly differentiated containing people of varying incomes and property ownership. They also contain squatters who rent out land they do not own but had previously claimed as their own. But instead of recognizing these realities, the advocates of community participation evoke a crude image of an élite that is separate from the 'real' community. While it is right that community participation should be concerned with issues of inequality, exploitation and oppression, a more refined analysis is needed. Similarly, because of their uncritical attitude, the proponents of community participation have failed to deal adequately with the problems of interpersonal relationships that arise in all communities. Even the most deprived sections of the community suffer from conflicts, rivalries and factionalism. A clearer understanding of these problems would allow a more realistic assessment of possibilities and prepare workers more adequately for the problems they will face.

The proponents of community participation are staunch advocates of local self-reliance, independence and autonomy and are stern critics of paternalism in all its guises. They have consistently attacked the 'top–down' approach of conventional community development and the efforts of external agencies to provide benevolently for the poor. However, they do not seem to realize that their own approach is riddled with paternalism. Although many writers claim that community workers always respect the community's right to decide its own affairs, it is unlikely that these workers will refrain from seeking to have their own views adopted. Indeed, the very act of introducing a community worker into the community as a part of a social development project or for any other motive is an external imposition. For all their protestations, the proponents of community participation are themselves guilty of a top–down or, at the very least, a laterally imposed form of intervention. This is most evident in publications dealing with poor people's alleged apathy and indifference to progress. The paternalism of the advocates of community participation is revealed also in their insistence that the only form of participation worth having is that which conforms to their own precepts. As was shown previously, traditional forms of participation, conventional local government and even political movements are dismissed as ineffectual.

Although many community participation advocates employ a concept of community participation that equates people's involvement with a total and continuous commitment to activism, this is hardly feasible. Studies of participation in political elections in the industrial countries give little scope for believing that intense long term mass involvement is likely. Ordinary people have many other commitments and it is a myth that the poor have an excess of free time. But this fact is often overlooked by the proponents of community participation who often complain about the failure of participatory programmes to secure indefinite and total involvement. As noted earlier, some have even despaired of revolutionary nationalist and socialist movements being able to sustain meaningful support. But it is surely unrealistic to hope for permanent activism or to conceive of community participation as an endless and hectic round of mass meetings, rallies, protests and other activities. Even revolutionaries will wish to resume the quiet life when they perceive that their struggle is won.

A more critical issue is whether or not community participation can achieve real improvements in social conditions. While some proponents of community participation believe that significant changes can be secured through popular involvement, others are surprisingly pessimistic. Many have laid down so many preconditions for successful participation that it is unlikely that they will ever be met. As noted earlier in this chapter, some have argued that profound social structural changes at both the domestic and international levels are necessary if community participation is to be effective. One advocate of community participation was not only doubtful about whether its principles would be widely adopted but 'whether such an approach can be implemented at all' (Galjart, 1981a, p. 88). Others are less pessimistic but nevertheless believe that community participation programmes will only contribute to social improvements in a small way (White, 1982).

However, doubts of this kind have been expressed not only by the advocates of community participation. There are critics of the approach as a whole who believe that real improvements in welfare flow not from community mobilization but rather from wider social and economic changes in society. Their views are invariably phrased in ideological terms invoking the arguments of established political beliefs which are reminiscent of older debates between anarchists, communists, socialists and liberals. While those on the right applaud the idea of self-reliance, they are not enamoured of the collectivist rhetoric of community participation. Also, they believe that the problems of mass poverty will not be eradicated by community activism but rather by the emergence of the values of individualism and competitive enterprise. On the other hand, socialists argue the case for state intervention and centralized planning. Although they do not oppose the idea of participation, they are sceptical of the claim that significant improvements in levels of living can be achieved through local development programmes. Marxists argue that it is only possible to bring about real improvements in welfare for the masses through the revolutionary transformation of society. Consequently, they do not participate in the debate between the proponents of centralism and community participation claiming that a discussion of possible reforms within the prevailing mode of production is a meaningless exercise.

Marxian writers have been major exponents of the idea that attempts at community participation are invariably subverted and neutralized by the state in capitalist societies. They argue that efforts by local people to organize themselves and to secure justice are perceived as a threat and are quickly suppressed. Sometimes this is done violently and brutally but often it is achieved through subtle manipulation. These writers believe that encounters between local people and the state result in the co-optation and emasculation of community effort. It is axiomatic, therefore, that they regard state sponsorship of community participation programmes as a contradiction in terms.

Community participation and the state

The view that government support for community participation in social development results not in an increase but in a diminution of community involvement is a paradox that is not often recognized. But it is widely held and even fashionable in development circles and is restated in the literature time and time again. On the other hand, some proponents of community participation have argued that state involvement is not only necessary but desirable. Hakim (1982, p. 140) claimed that community participation is dependent on 'services that only government can provide'. Similarly, UNICEF (1982) believes that community social development programmes are often ineffective without government support. There are other views on this question. Some authors claim that state support can be helpful but that local people must be taught how to resist the efforts of bureaucrats and politicians to subvert their authority. Others believe that bureaucrats and politicians are not hostile to community participation but that the complexities of modern societies and the formalized procedures of government mitigate against popular involvement.

Different views of state involvement in community participation mirror wider beliefs about the nature of state power in modern societies. As was shown in the introduction to this book, there are a variety of social science theories of the contemporary state which evoke different images of state–society relationships. While Marxian and élite theories are pessimistic about the possibility of community participation, liberal-democratic and pluralist theories are much more hopeful. Although implicit, these theories have informed different views of state involvement in community participation. But just as no theory of the state is fully accepted, so no account of state–community relations in social development commands universal support. Indeed, it is obvious that a variety of interpretations is possible.

It is theoretically feasible to construct a typology of explanations of state responses to community participation. The state's attitude may be classified in terms of various criteria including its definition of what participation entails, its perception of the possibility of instability and the degree to which it is willing to devolve power to local political institutions. Obviously, there are many more. In the following examination of state responses to community participation, four ideal typical modes may be identified and, in addition, there are several variants of each.

The anti-participatory mode

The first mode is congruent with Marxian and élite theories which hold that the state is not interested in the poor and that it supports neither community participation nor social development. Instead, the state acts on behalf of the ruling class, furthering their interests, the accumulation of wealth and the concentration of power. Efforts to mobilize the masses for participation will be seen as a threat and suppressed.

Some proponents of this explanation of state responses to community participation qualify their arguments to suggest that the primary impediment to participation is the capitalist system itself and that once a revolutionary transformation of society has taken place, mechanisms for the full participation of the people and the realization of their aspirations will emerge. Others do not make this explicit but, by referring to the achievements of countries such as China and Cuba, they imply that communist societies offer real opportunities for grass-roots involvement. Hollnsteiner (1982a) argued, for example, that in contrast to the community based development strategies of China, Ethiopia, Tanzania and Vietnam, capitalist Third World countries are unlikely to become organized for self-reliant development. Numerous authors have cited the Chinese commune as an ideal form of participation which not only offers its members full democratic rights but promotes effective social development.

But it is certainly not universally accepted that authentic community participation can only occur in communist societies. Indeed, a definitive statement on this question was issued at a meeting of delegates from thirty-seven countries and ten United Nations agencies in Ljubljana, Yugoslavia in 1982 which concluded that the ideals of community participation are universal 'regardless of whether a self-proclaimed socialist, capitalist or distinctive system is being described' (Smith, 1982, p. 166). Others have pointed out that community participation programmes have been established in many non-socialist countries. Even in Latin America, which is characterized by widespread authoritarianism, they believed that 'the region offers favourable conditions for the promotion of social movements as a forum of expression of popular demands and participation in society' (Pearse and Stiefel, 1979, p. 165).

Liberal sympathizers of Third World communist governments do not always recognize that these are self-proclaimed totalitarian regimes which offer few opportunities for a free expression of views. Nor do they appreciate the apparent paradox that participation is most likely in liberal societies where pluralist beliefs are institutionalized. Revelations of the misuse of power in communist societies such as Ethiopia, Poland and the Soviet Union hardly support the argument that these governments are paragons of participatory sponsorship. It is also the case, as Wolfe (1982) observed, that post-revolutionary regimes often resort to the same anti-participatory tactics they previously opposed and that a new class of functionaries emerges to wield power and manipulate grass-roots movements. Although there are many governments in the Third World today that have actively suppressed participatory movements, these oppressive regimes do not govern the majority of the world's nation states. The most notorious, which include military dictatorships in Chile and elsewhere, the murderous Khmer Rouge and the family dynasties of Haiti and Somozan Nicaragua have become notorious and it is right that their brutal suppression of human freedoms should be condemned. Although it cannot be claimed that the governments of the developing nations are wholly committed to social development and welfare, it would also be wrong to argue that there are no prospects for further improvements in social conditions.

The manipulative mode

In this second mode, the state supports community participation but does so for ulterior motives. Among these are a desire to use community participation for purposes of political and social control and a recognition that community participation can reduce the costs of social development programmes and facilitate implementation. This view of the state's response to community participation is influenced by both élitist and corporatist theory which emphasizes the capacity of the state to subvert and co-opt autonomous movements and to preserve its own power. Although genuine social benefits may accrue to the poor, they nevertheless remain dependent on the 'top–down' transfer of resources and fail to realize their potential for autonomous co-operative action.

Many authorities have warned of the dangers of co-optation. This is defined as a process by which the state seeks to gain control over grass-roots movements and to manipulate them for its own ends. Of course, the state may seek to co-opt participatory groups to varying degrees and for different reasons. At one extreme is an attempt to neutralize potential opposition which is so sinister that it constitutes an anti-participatory response. At the other extreme, co-optation may occur inadvertently as a part of the formalization of routine exchanges between civil servants and community leaders. Co-optation may also occur because the state seeks to direct participatory aspirations through alternative mechanisms which it has established and which it regards as legitimate and satisfactory. These may include political institutions such as the Basic Democracies of Pakistan or the People's Congresses of Libya. Although the state does not oppose community involvement, it seeks to neutralize spontaneous participatory activities hoping to channel them through established mechanisms. One mechanism of this kind, which is often regarded as the primary institution for participation in totalitarian political systems, is the ruling political party itself.

In many Third World countries, ruling élites cannot conceive of any form of popular participation outside the structures of the party apparatus. Bugnicourt (1982) has encountered this attitude in Africa. In one case, officials told local people that since the party was the 'Party of the People', their spontaneous efforts at community participation must be channelled through the party. But, as he argued, the claim of political parties to express the democratic aspirations of the masses 'most often reflects hierarchically transmitted impulses' (p. 67).

Another form of manipulative participation occurs when the state sponsors community participation for instrumental reasons. Many governments employ the rhetoric of participation to recruit labour for development projects without involving the people in decision-making. The proponents of community participation condemn this practice not only because it is undemocratic and suppresses local initiative but because it often leads to abuse. There are many cases of coerced participation which have caused great resentment. As Mould's (1966) study of community development in Sierra Leone revealed, the attempts of local officials and chiefs to compel the people to participate in government projects was violently opposed and had negative repercussions for the programme.

The state may also foster participatory activities as a part of its efforts to extend social and political control over the population. Since participatory rhetoric may encourage ordinary people to identify with national political ideologies, give legitimacy to ruling élites and help to integrate marginal communities into the social and political system, community participation principles may well appeal to governments. Again, party functionaries play a key role in implementing this approach.

The incremental mode

The incremental mode is characterized by official support for community participation ideas but also by a *laissez-faire* or ambivalent approach to implementation that fails to support local activities properly or to ensure that participatory institutions function effectively. In this mode, state politics are usually vaguely formulated, poorly implemented and lacking in determination. It is congruent with a widespread incrementalist approach to social administration in the Third World (Hardiman and Midgley, 1982) in which governments do not formulate comprehensive social policies preferring instead to 'muddle through' on an *ad hoc* basis towards the attainment of loosely formulated social development goals. This response to community participation is associated with pluralist political ideas but it is also found in societies with strong central governments. While these governments do not oppose community participation, they fail to provide the necessary backing to ensure its realization.

Incremental responses to community participation may also be an expression of a genuine political ambivalence about the viability of community based social development programmes. Ambivalence characterizes the views of political élites who regard community participation as worthy but believe, at the same time, that the problems of Third World countries require concerted central government action which overrides local interests. This view

characterizes the socialist attitude which approves of local participation and self-reliance but believes, nevertheless, that solutions to
national development problems cannot be found locally. Since
socialist policy will be directed towards the strengthening of the state
and the promotion of central planning, community participation will
suffer and the state's response may well be incrementalist in
character.

A far more common cause of incremental community participation
is policy and administrative ineffectiveness. Many government
sponsored community participation programmes fail because of the
sheer inertia of the centralized state apparatus with its bureaucratic
procedures, inefficiency, inflexibility and remoteness. Many writers
have singled out this problem as the major impediment to effective
community participation in the Third World. The United Nations
(1981) observed that the tendency towards centralization in many
developing countries has created a complex administrative system
that is inimical to community participation. Hollnsteiner (1977)
pointed out that the complexities of administering modern societies
have fostered the emergence of a technocracy of experts that has
great difficulty in understanding or interacting with local people.
Middle-class technocrats cannot easily accept that near illiterate
peasants or slum dwellers can make an effective contribution to social
development policy. Nor are they likely to support measures that will
weaken their authority, question their expertise or threaten their
interests. If community participation has this effect, it is likely that
they will seek to undermine participatory activities. As Wolfe (1982)
observed, even an efficient, goal orientated and honest bureaucracy
will experience tension in dealing with community groups. Also, the
United Nations (1975a) pointed out that administrators and policy
makers are rightly concerned with norms of efficiency and accomp-
lishment that may be adversely affected by community participation.
The conflict between community participation ideals and administrative efficiency frequently mitigates against the emergence of the
type of participatory mode advocated in the literature on community
participation.

The participatory mode

In this mode, the state approves fully of community participation and
responds by creating mechanisms for the effective involvement of

local communities in all aspects of development. Inspired by various social and political theories including populism, anarchism and pluralism, the participatory mode involves a real devolution of power. In addition to creating genuine community level political institutions, the state sponsors participatory activities through the training and deployment of community workers, the provision of material and other forms of assistance and the co-ordination of central, regional and local decisions through comprehensive national planning. A concerted effort is made to enfranchise the poorest sections of the community and recognition and support is provided for voluntary associations of all kinds. Local decision-making bodies are given specific rights and functions and real control over budgets. Steps are taken to ensure that civil servants are sensitized to the needs of ordinary people and that participation becomes institutionalized in the administrative procedures of government. Above all, major economic and social reforms are carried out to ensure that poor communities derive real benefits from national development effort and that political participation and social development ideals are integrated.

It is, of course, the hope of the proponents of community participation that their efforts will result in Third World governments adopting the participatory stance. The remainder of this book will seek to discover whether there is scope for optimism and whether progress has been made towards the realization of the participatory mode in social development.

PART II

2

People's involvement in health and medical care

MARGARET HARDIMAN

The declaration on 'Health for all by the year 2000' made at the International Conference on Primary Health Care at Alma Ata in September 1978 drew attention to the widespread lack of facilities for large numbers of people in the world today. Despite considerable progress many problems remain and national policies for the most part have so far proved inadequate to tackle them effectively.

The stress on the priority that should be given to primary health care is not new. For many years before Alma Ata, health planners were advocating alternative policies with this emphasis, as is demonstrated by the writings of Colbourne (1963), Titmuss (1964), King (1970) and Gish (1970). Doctors dealing with health problems at grass-roots level had been particularly insistent on the benefits to be gained from involving the community, and had already written on this theme (Flavier, 1970; Arole, 1972; Morley, 1973). The World Health Organization's publication *Health by the People* edited by Newell (1975) brought together articles by a group of persons from many countries who were close to the villagers themselves.

This then is an area in which community participation has for long been advocated, and if health services are considered in the broadest sense to include environmental aspects such as good water supplies, sanitation and nutrition, then the need for participation is clear. The history of industrialization in the nineteenth century, accompanied as it was by appalling living conditions in the new towns, provided ample proof of the ineffectiveness of curative medicine in the face of poor sanitation and water supplies. And in the industrialized countries today, with their sophisticated medical services, there is increasing realization that health cannot be secured by the provision of medical care alone; much more attention is now being paid to environmental and behavioural aspects. One of the lessons from this experience is that better health care is not just a question of spending more money on services. Finance is important, but its effectiveness depends on how it is used, and what the response is from those it plans to benefit (Abel-Smith, 1976). It is, for example, no use digging a tube well to provide clean water supply if householders collect and store the water in contaminated pots.

Before considering the question of how to use community participation as a strategy, this chapter will look briefly at the situation of health and health services in the Third World today. It will then consider alternative approaches to state health care policies and trace the history of ideas about participation asking questions about the different ways in which they are understood and implemented. The use of participatory methods will be illustrated by selected case studies. In conclusion, the lessons to be learnt from these experiences will be discussed with a view to showing the possibilities and limitations of community participation.

Health and health services in the Third World

There have been undoubted improvements during the past 20 to 30 years in life expectancy, which is one of the main indicators used to measure the health status of a country. There have also been gains in the control of epidemic diseases, notably smallpox which has virtually been eradicated. In line with these improvements, infant mortality rates, another key indicator, have fallen. The reliability of data on vital statistics is poor for most developing countries, and because information is collected in many different ways with varying degrees of accuracy, cross country comparisons are dangerous. Infant mortality rates are especially prone to error; a higher rate may merely mean that there is a more efficient system of recording. But despite these doubts, the trend in most countries shows a considerable improvement in these indicators.

Table 2.1 Life expectancy and infant mortality in selected developing countries

Country	Life expectancy at birth (years) 1960	1980	Infant mortality per 1000 1960	1980
Chad	35	41	195	149
Bangladesh	37	46	159	136
Ethiopia	36	40	175	146
Zaire	40	47	150	112
Malawi	37	44	207	172
Mozambique	37	47	160	115
India	43	52	165	123
Haiti	44	53	182	115
Pakistan	43	50	162	126
Uganda	44	54	139	97
Benin	37	47	206	154
Ghana	40	49	143	103
Kenya	41	55	138	87
Indonesia	46	58	148	88
Zambia	40	49	151	106
Bolivia	43	50	167	131
El Salvador	51	63	136	78
Cameroon	37	47	162	109
Thailand	52	63	103	55
Peru	47	58	163	88
Nigeria	39	49	183	136
Jamaica	64	71	52	16
Cuba	63	73	66	21
Korea	54	65	78	34
Costa Rica	62	70	71	24
Algeria	47	56	165	118

Source: World Bank (1982)

The improvements in life expectancy have been accompanied by a rise in the physician and nurse population ratios, and an increase in the proportion of people with access to safe water supplies. Table 2.1 and Table 2.2 illustrate the position in selected developing countries and are interesting not only for showing the changes over the past twenty years, but for the wide variations between countries.

There are significant differences between the industrialized and

Community Participation, Social Development and the State

Table 2.2 Population per physician ratio and access to safe water in selected developing countries

Country	Population per physician no. 1960	1977	Percentage with access to safe drinking water 1975
Chad	72,000	41,000	26
Bangladesh	—	12,000	53
Ethiopia	100,000	74,000	6
Zaire	37,000	15,000	16
Malawi	35,000	41,000	33
Mozambique	20,000	35,000	—
India	4,000	3,600	33
Haiti	9,200	5,900	14
Pakistan	5,400	3,700	29
Uganda	15,000	26,000	35
Benin	23,000	26,000	21
Ghana	21,000	9,000	35
Kenya	10,000	11,600	17
Indonesia	46,000	13,000	12
Zambia	9,500	10,400	42
Bolivia	3,800	1,800	34
El Salvador	5,200	3,600	53
Cameroon	48,000	16,000	26
Thailand	7,900	8,200	22
Peru	2,100	1,500	48
Nigeria	73,000	15,000	—
Jamaica	2,500	3,500	86
Cuba	1,000	1,100	—
Korea	3,500	1,900	71
Costa Rica	2,700	1,300	77
Algeria	5,500	5,300	77

Source: World Bank (1982)

the developing countries in the causes of mortality and morbidity. Table 2.3 illustrates this for two industrial and two developing countries and shows a typical pattern in mortality trends. Communicable diseases are still the prevailing cause of death in the Third World and this also applies to the incidence of diseases which, although they may not kill, have an adverse effect on human

48

Table 2.3 Percentage of deaths attributed to different diseases in selected countries, 1978

Cause of death	Mexico	Philippines	Canada	Italy
All communicable diseases	15.3	22.3	0.5	0.7
Malignant neoplasms	5.8	4.9	22.0	21.4
Ischaemic heart disease	3.4	4.2	31.1	17.1

Source: United Nations (1984)

growth, well-being and efficiency. One reason for the sharp contrast between the industrialized and developing countries is the difference in the age distribution of the population and the particular vulnerability of young children in the Third World. In industrialized countries, not more than about 21 per cent of the population is under 15 years of age, whereas in many developing countries, this applies to nearly 50 per cent. As can be seen from Table 2.1, infant mortality rates are still high in many developing countries. Maternal mortality and child death rates are also at an unacceptably high level, quite apart from the effects on the health of both mother and child of poor nutrition, living conditions and multiple pregnancies (Morley and Woodland, 1979; Shah, 1981).

The vast majority of the health problems from which people in developing countries suffer are connected with endemic environmental conditions such as poor sanitation, unsafe water and inadequate food supplies, particularly when seasonal variations are taken into account (Chambers, 1981). They are problems which can best be tackled by prevention and by simple treatments rather than sophisticated medical techniques. Moreover, they are problems which can only be effectively overcome by involving the people themselves in health care programmes and environmental improvement schemes.

State health policies and alternative approaches

In most developing countries health policies have been modelled as far as medical care is concerned on those of the industrialized nations, but without the same degree of attention that has been given in the developed world to environmental services such as good water supplies, sanitation and housing standards. Nor has there been the same insistence on preventive measures, particularly with regard to the protection of children against epidemic and infectious diseases by immunization. The emphasis on curative medicine and the limitation of environmental services to areas where Europeans lived is to some extent a legacy of colonial times. On gaining independence new nations were determined that their people should benefit from the obviously effective treatments provided by modern medicine. But too little account was taken by governments of the nature of the health problems confronting them, and this resulted in a concentration on curative services that were expensive and available only to a small proportion of the population, a phenomenon that has been well documented (Abel-Smith, 1976; Gish, 1970; King, 1966; Malcolm, 1978, to mention only a few) and has led to the present insistence on the need for primary health care being made a priority.

Planners in many developing countries have responded to this problem by putting forward proposals for wider coverage of the population with the use of more appropriate methods. Examples of this are the document prepared by the Planning Unit of the Ministry of Health in Zambia, in the foreword to which the Minister states that 'Social justice demands a major change in the nation's health system, so that all the people have access to effective health care' (Zambia, 1980, p. 1), or the Indian Government Report on 'Health for All by 2000 AD' (India, 1981). Despite these sentiments budgetary allocations offer little promise that the proposals can be implemented to more than a limited extent. This is a real dilemma facing Third World countries. They have already created sophisticated curative systems, where a large proportion of the budget goes to hospitals. The demand for these services is great and any government attempting to curtail them would be severely criticized by the most articulate and influential sections of society. Moreover the medical profession is unlikely to support a radical change in policy if it sees its position threatened by financial cuts on the curative section. As with all questions related to social policies it is easier to suggest alternatives than to implement them. Unless there is a fundamental change in the social structure alternative policies may only be accepted if they are seen by those in power either to be necessary in order to maintain their position, or to be sufficiently low cost, effective and of popular appeal. Health is an area where some pressure does exist from international agencies through the publication of comparative health statistics and survey findings. Because of its relation to the perceived problem of population growth the case for rethinking can be seen as strong. As population pressures increase, particularly in countries with very high rates of growth, such as Kenya and elsewhere in Africa, the urgency of the situation may result in policies being adopted which benefit health services more generally.

From all that has been said it is evident that a much higher priority given to environmental services is likely to be an extremely cost-effective method of improving a nation's health. But even if this is agreed in principle by governments questions arise as to how measures can best be financed and delivered. At present there is an urban bias in the provision of services. People living in a town expect the municipality to provide water, sewerage, refuse disposal, street cleaning and so forth. They may have to pay a rate, or tax for these services, but they are unlikely to be called on to participate, except perhaps in squatter areas where self-help projects are mounted. In rural areas many governments have relied on community development principles in the provision of services. Villages have been expected to provide at least a part of the expense of improving water supplies and sanitation. This has on the one hand been described as a laudable way of securing community involvement, and on the other as a means of saving government expenditure in rural areas so that more can be spent in cities. However, in the poorest countries, where existing provisions are minimal, the cost of providing adequate services on a nationwide basis by conventional methods is undoubtedly beyond their means.

This has led international agencies, well aware of the significance of environmental factors, to consider the possibilities of using overseas aid. Assistance with improving water supply and sanitation has become an essential part of the development strategy of such bodies as the World Health Organization, UNDP, the World Bank as well as by voluntary organizations such as OXFAM. Increasingly these agencies, however, are realizing that it is not enough just to provide money to build pipelines, dig wells or erect latrines. If these measures are to be effective much more thought has to be given to the cultural situation of the communities concerned. Problems of design and delivery should be discussed with the people before decisions are taken, and the people should be involved throughout the whole project. Ultimately, the good use and maintenance of services will largely depend on them and this must be taken into account at the design stage. Proper attention to these details will not only ensure a successful outcome but will probably save a great deal of money. The case of China is a good example of how very simple measures can be effective if they are understood by the community.

From this it is clear that environmental health is an area in which community participation is essential, and that priority must be given to undertaking how best it can be secured. Only then can appropriate policies be formulated. One lesson from this is that much greater flexibility is needed in order to cope with variations between and within different regions of a country; what will work, for example, in southern Ghana may not be at all appropriate in the north.

Appropriate medical care policies require the adoption of both preventive and curative measures and this raises the question of the role of different personnel. What level of medical professional should be used and in what capacity? Is there a place for the non-medical person and if so, in what way?

Table 2.2 shows that there are not enough doctors in developing countries to provide all the medical care needed. In fact the position is far worse than indicated, as the majority of doctors live in towns. In India, for example, where the doctor/population ratio is better than in many countries, roughly 80 per cent of the doctors practise in towns, whereas 80 per cent of the population lives in rural areas.

One remedy suggested has been to redistribute doctors, either by compulsion, or by offering differential salaries and conditions of service. Certainly more doctors are needed in rural areas, and to serve the most deprived parts of large cities but this strategy alone is not likely to reach the masses of most countries in the foreseeable future. The poorer countries cannot afford to employ doctors on this scale, so that even if steps are taken to redeploy them and to halt emigration the problem will not be resolved. The solution must therefore be found elsewhere.

The use of nurses and medical auxiliaries has for long been advocated (ITDG, 1971, which cites much of the earlier literature on this subject; Gish, 1977; Hetzel, 1978) and where they have been used they have been found to make a valuable contribution to health care. In French-speaking areas of Africa the idea is far from new; the training of medical auxiliaries has formed an integral part of the system of medical education. And in the industrialized countries there has been a trend towards supplementing the services of doctors with nursing and other personnel. For example, in the UK, the Gillie sub-committee in 1963 suggested that domiciliary nursing staff should be attached to family doctors and attachment schemes have now been introduced by many local health services. These schemes are not an attempt to relieve the general practitioner of responsibility, but to make more effective use of both medical and nursing skills to meet the needs of the community.

In Russia there is a long history of using auxiliaries, going back to the introduction by Peter the Great in 1700 of a corps of military feldshers (field barbers) who were trained to provide medical care to the army. After demobilization many feldshers returned to rural areas where they continued to practise their skills amongst local people. After the Revolution there was an attempt to upgrade the more skilled feldshers to doctor status and to stop training auxiliaries, but despite the big increase in the number of doctors, auxiliaries continue to be needed and remain an important part of both urban and rural medical care in the USSR (ITDG, 1971).

The value of using auxiliaries is self-evident from a financial point of view. Their training and remuneration are much lower. But they are also, because of the type of training and their position in the community, likely to be more effective in meeting the needs of the people. It has been found in England that where a nurse is attached to a family doctor, patients, once they are aware of what she can do, prefer her services for certain aspects of medical care, such as home visiting and advice on the care of young children.

In developing countries where medical auxiliaries have been used it has frequently been found that even these have not reached down to the grass-roots problems of the vast majority. There are many reasons for this. For one thing it is not possible to provide enough personnel to cover every village in rural areas, nor every squatter settlement in towns. Moreover the type of person trained does not always settle happily in a village situation. In India, for example, it has been found that auxiliary nurse midwives when posted to remote villages have often found their position intolerable, and have spent most of their time away from their station on various pretexts.

The alternative strategy that has been developed is to use village people themselves as health workers. The great advantage of this is that the worker belongs to the community and understands its way of life. This method of providing medical care has been widely acclaimed in the past few years (WHO, 1982) and is now being adopted as government policy in many countries. It is too early to assess how universally effective it is likely to be, but some lessons can already be learnt from projects which have made use of such workers (Werner, 1977). Not only is it essential to have a good system of training; there must be constant follow-up, supervision and encouragement. The backing of the community must be assured and must continue to operate after the initial enthusiasm. The demise of many projects after early success bears testimony to the results of neglecting these criteria.

The idea of participation

Although only recently popularized this idea is not new. Many of the strategies outlined above had been tried in the 1920s and 1930s, for example by doctors like B. B. Waddy in Ghana, who virtually eliminated river-blindness by training young men from the affected villages to follow up treatment, or by district officers such as Brayne (1929) in the Punjab, who understood the importance of involving village people, particularly women, in improving their living conditions. Many of the remedies advocated strike a familiar note. Brayne, for example, stressed the importance of integrated village development; health could not be improved without attention to agricultural development, nothing could be effective unless the co-operation of village people was assured. He understood from experience that the approach of officials to village people was fraught with difficulties. It was only after many years that he appreciated just how suspicious villagers were of officialdom, because so often the official had a sting in his tail. This could only be overcome by working continuously with rural people over a long period, getting to know their problems at first hand and gaining their confidence. But Brayne also pointed out that sufficient funds must be made available by government if there was to be any real progress. This has perhaps continued to be the crux of the matter.

To cite from India again. Even as far back as 1946, the Bhore Committee (India, 1946) mentioned, in its recommendations, access to the poor, rural priorities, comprehensive care with community based rather than hospital based services, self-responsibility of the citizen for his own health and the doctor as a social physician. Unfortunately, however, there is a wide gap between what is professed and planned and its implementation (John, 1982; ICSSR/ICMR, 1981; Karkal, 1982).

The case of China is a well known example of the success of participatory methods in raising health standards. China in the 1930s and 1940s suffered from widespread poverty, poor sanitation and rampant disease, with an estimated one in five of all babies born dying in the first five years of life. Preventive medicine was almost non-existent and medical care was mainly provided by practitioners of traditional medicine ranging from poorly educated pill peddlers to well-trained, widely experienced practitioners (Sidel and Sidel, 1975, p. 2). When Mao and the Chinese Communist Party assumed power in 1949 one of the elements of their health policy was that 'Health work should be conducted with mass participation – that is, everyone in the society was to be encouraged to play an organized role in the protection of his own health and that of his neighbours' (Sidel and Sidel, 1975, p. 3). The practical implementation of this policy has been impressive, a classic example being the success of the campaign against schistosomiasis, based on the concept of a 'mass line'. This involved a thorough education of the people on the subject of the disease, with lectures, films, posters and radio talks. Twice a year everybody was mobilized to drain rivers and ditches and to take other steps to fight against the snails. Conquering the problem was not easy; it meant many years of hard work in the first place and constant vigilance thereafter. The important lesson was that it showed what could be done by co-operation and an understanding of the problem (Horn, 1971).

The schistosomiasis campaign is a good example of the effectiveness of mass organization. It certainly involves the participation of the people. But the initiative in this case came from above. The people were told what to do; they were not involved in decision-making as to how to set about it. There is nothing wrong about this, as the people were the ultimate beneficiaries of the campaign. And the campaign itself was set in the context of a society with a strong ideological commitment to improvement along prescribed lines. But the same methods might not meet with such success in a different socio-political setting. China is a controlled society to a high degree. The extent of mass participation is impressive, but it involves perceiving the freedom of the individual in a very different light from that in western countries. The methods used may well be more appropriate to many developing countries which share similar views about the role of the individual, although there are other factors at work which may limit the extent of replicability. An interesting example is the one-child family policy at present being pursued in China; strong pressures are being put on women to conform to this norm, so far apparently without any mass revolt against the harsh measures often involved, such as abortion at a late stage of pregnancy. It is difficult to imagine such programmes meeting with success elsewhere. The prospect of forced sterilization in India during the Emergency is considered to have contributed to the downfall of Mrs Gandhi's government.

Chapter 1 discussed the different meanings and types of community participation, and asked questions about the form participation takes, who is involved and for what purpose. Applied to the field of health it can on the one hand be used to describe the mobilization of the community as in the schistosomiasis campaign in China. This undoubtedly involved the people, and there are some aspects of environmental and preventive health where initiative may have to come from above in the first place.

But community participation can go much further into the field of decision-making, even if the initiative again comes from outside. The example of the Arole's programme at Jamkhed in India (Arole, 1972, 1975) is one such case. The Aroles wanted to improve health care in the villages around Jamkhed; but before designing their programme they went out to consult the people. How did they perceive their health problem? What were their priority needs? They were interested to find that the villagers' main concern was with water and food supplies, so they started with these, and through this mobilized the community into an active programme which later extended to medical care. As this developed they identified and used local personnel and their eventual reliance on the village health worker as the lynch-pin of the programme has been widely acclaimed. She is selected by the village people themselves, is herself a part of the community, and through her work has gained the respect and confidence of the people. But it is important to stress that her effectiveness also depends on the continuing support and encouragement of the project as a whole, and that the treatments she can offer depend on the expertise of highly qualified doctors and their commitment to the improvement of rural health.

Participation in this sense means listening to the people, taking them into account in the design of projects and programmes, and relying on them in the implementation process. Both in this case and even where more cavalier methods of participation are used, understanding the community is an essential ingredient. Nothing can be taken for granted; no one community is exactly like another, so community involvement requires a flexibility of approach if it is to be effective. Where the initiative comes from outside it is necessary to know the leadership pattern and how far different groups participate in traditional forms of decision-making. In many cases some categories are entirely left out, such as women or harijans (untouchables) in India. If participation by the community as a whole is to be achieved special tactics may have to be used. It is easy enough, for example, to go into an African village, have long and seemingly fruitful talks with the chief and elders, without any idea as to how far their views represent the interests of the people as a whole.

Another question concerns the relationship between participation and self-sufficiency or self-reliance. Whether or not the initial impetus comes from outside, should projects aim at handing over to local communities at a specified time? For example, in the case of Jamkhed the villages select their health workers, but the stipends are paid by the project. There is much controversy on this point, some believing that villages should pay for their workers themselves. But even if this were done, to what extent could a scattered group of villagers sustain the organizational and referral centre necessary for a comprehensive health project of this type? Could they set up the administrative framework necessary to employ doctors and nurses, order equipment and so forth? In other words, could they run the programme on a co-operative basis? This chapter will return to these questions after considering the case studies.

Participation in action

The case studies have been chosen as examples of where participation in some form has proved successful. Inevitably they are taken from relatively small-scale projects, as outside China and Cuba it is these which have used this approach to the greatest extent. But if participation is to be used to make a real impact on health standards they must be replicable and governments must incorporate the strategies in their programmes in a more meaningful way than hitherto.

The Kasa mother–child health-nutrition project

A special interest of this case study is that the project was sponsored by the Government of India, and the State Government of Maharashtra, and that the organizational structure was within the normal pattern of government health services for rural areas, based as they are on the Primary Health Centres. The additional inputs were provided by CARE-Maharashtra, which administered the project and by Professor P. M. Shah, the Technical Project Director of the Institute of Child Health in Bombay. The project goal was 'to establish the administrative feasibility of adopting for large-scale government implementation an integrated approach to the problems of rural pre-school and maternal health and nutrition' (Shah, 1976, p. 3). It was proposed that local villagers should be used to identify problem families and that implementation should involve community participation. Reports on the project were written by Professor Shah and are extremely frank about the limitations and problems that arose, as well as the successes.

The Kasa project which started in 1975 was located in northern Maharashtra in Thana District, which had a population of 74,500 dispersed in seventy-nine villages. Eighty-eight per cent of the population was tribal, the per capita income was extremely low at less than one rupee a day (comparisons are not very meaningful, but at the time £1 sterling = 16 rupees), and the level of literacy was about 11 per cent of all adults. Villages were scattered over a wide area (475 sq. km), roads were poor, there was no telephone or telegraph and only a few villages had electricity. Twenty-one per cent out of seventy-nine project villages were inaccessible by vehicle for half the year, due to lack of bridge crossings of seasonal rivers.

The first stage of participation in the project involved the workers at the Primary Health Centre (PHC), that is the medical officers, the eight auxiliary nurse midwives (two at headquarters and six in sub-centres) and four smallpox vaccinators. It was intended that all the medical auxiliaries should be converted into multi-purpose health workers. The approach and objectives were fully explained at a joint meeting, the implications were discussed and finally the job assignments and areas of service were agreed. Professor Shah in his reports gives much credit to the tireless efforts of the staff, their support and co-operation. They themselves were enthusiastic about the opportunity to work as a team on a project whose aims they understood and in the implementation of which their views were continually sought.

The second stage of participation was at community level. At the onset of the project the programme was explained to the local communities. The villages were asked to suggest candidates to act as part-time social workers (PTSWs), the role of the PTSWs being to bridge the gap between the multi-purpose health workers on the staff of the PHC and the community. The method of using PTSWs for this purpose had already been tried by Shah in a project at Palghar, Maharashtra, for the Domiciliary Treatment of Malnutrition, and it had been found highly successful.

Although it was originally envisaged that PTSWs would be middle-aged mothers with about seven years of schooling, communities were not able to find a sufficient number of suitable women of this type. In the event over 50 per cent of the PTSWs were males, and their mean age was about twenty-two years. Perhaps because of these initial difficulties the drop-out rate was heavy. It might have been better, as was done in the Jamkhed project, not to insist on literacy, particularly in a tribal area with such low levels of education. As a result of adopting this policy the involvement of women was not as great as it might have been.

The initial training period lasted four weeks, and was practical in nature, with time spent in the field. PTSWs were taught to use weight charts, identify kwashiorkor, severe anaemia, vitamin A deficiency and to assess the grade of malnutrition. After the initial training PTSWs were brought in to the PHC at frequent intervals for further training to consolidate and extend their skills. For example in the second year of the project it was decided that family planning programmes would be introduced, after vital support had been obtained from local bodies such as the Panchayat Samiti (a local body at block level) and the Forest Workers' Society, both of whom provided generous cash donations.

Because this was an experimental project emphasis was put on research into the impact of the approach used. This proved a very difficult exercise in the Kasa area, as accurate base data was lacking and could not be collected from all the villages with the resources available. However, for those components that could be measured a satisfactory degree of success was recorded. Particularly successful was the acceptance of immunization; for example at the beginning of the project only 10.2 per cent of the children had been given BCG vaccines, whereas at the end of one year this went up to 57 per cent. In view of the terrain of the area and the sizeable tribal population this was a remarkable achievement and shows the extent of rapport that PTSWs had developed with the villagers. Participation in the nutrition programme was also good in most communities. PTSWs were involved in stimulating more 'self-help' by meeting with villagers, telling them of the nutritional status of their children and listing the names of those 'at risk' who required special care. In many cases solutions were suggested by the villagers themselves and individuals offered to provide sites on their verandahs where nutrition supplements could be distributed. In several cases, milk was provided by villagers to mothers who had lactation failure.

Many other instances of community help could be cited, such as co-operation over road construction to ease communications with the PHC. As well the project did manage to secure much more active participation from communities in improving their own health. Shah (1976) believed, however, in assessing the programmes that more still might have been done if the approach had been widened to include other aspects of health, such as the improvement of water supply, environmental sanitation and income-raising activities. In the third report, Shah (1977) expressed concern about community support, which had not been forthcoming in some respects to the degree that would be desirable. 'Some of the explanation', he said 'may lie in the fact that preventive health programmes do not meet a felt need, and in fact may seem foreign and imposed on the population. Only education can change this viewpoint to develop awareness and concern for the community's well-being as a whole' (Shah, 1977, p. 57). Local leaders had supported the PTSWs and had co-operated in many other ways, but the main body of villagers themselves had been slow to offer active assistance, such as by helping to collect children for weighing or in supervising feeding. This may have been due to widespread poverty; basic food requirements were of paramount concern, so that health care or development activities may have been viewed as secondary in importance. But this does illustrate the need to take all the people into account, not just to appeal to the leaders.

Although the Kasa project can be considered successful in achieving some of its major objectives it has not served as an organizational model for replication throughout Maharashtra. The strategy of using part-time village health workers has, however, been adopted as state policy, although it is too early to assess how effective it will be in different circumstances.

The Serabu Hospital village health project

This project was initiated by a Roman Catholic church hospital at Serabu, a village of 2500 people in the Southern Province of Sierra Leone (Ross, 1979). It is an area of poor, farming communities where there are high rates of infant mortality (over 200:2000 in the mid-1970s) and child mortality. The birth rate for Sierra Leone at the time was estimated at 45:1000, and the death rate at 20:1000, life expectancy was low at about 45 years and nearly 40 per cent of the population was under 15 years of age. The main health problems were endemic environmental diseases, malaria, diarrhoea, tetanus and hookworm.

In 1966 Serabu Hospital had started to operate a mobile clinic of the standard maternal and child health pattern, at first serving villages within a 25 km range and later more distant communities. In 1975 the programme was reviewed partly because of its cost, both to the hospital and the rural communities, but mainly because the staff could see little improvement in the health of the people, despite their efforts. Since the hospital had to rely on charging fees to patients for 80 per cent of its budget the poorer families tended to stay away or only seek help at a late and often fatal stage of an illness. Moreover even when cured many patients returned with the same complaint after a short period; this was commonest for hookworm and other intestinal parasites, child malnutrition and tuberculosis.

A great deal of thought went into planning an alternative strategy which would deal more effectively with local health problems. In 1975 a sample survey was carried out in seven villages to determine local mortality and morbidity patterns. The results confirmed that most of the diseases recorded were preventable by better sanitation, improved hygiene, or immunization and were treatable by simple, inexpensive means.

Already the people had been involved in helping the team with the survey, and were beginning to understand better the underlying causes of their problems. Every attempt had been made to involve traditional health personnel, particularly the traditional birth attendants who were influential members of the women's 'Bundu Sande', the women's secret society. Members of Sande were traditionally responsible for maternal and child health, nutrition, domestic hygiene and herbal medicine. The adult men of the villages all belonged to the 'Bundu Poro' (the men's secret society) and it was their traditional responsibility to look after the water supply, rubbish disposal, defecation, and environmental hygiene. The village health project therefore based itself on the indigenous social structure using local people to extend the roles which they already performed.

The proposal was that the scheme should work through a village health committee, selected by each village itself and meeting with hospital staff at least once a month. This committee would be responsible for discussing methods of improving health by disease prevention, and carrying out decisions reached with the help of other villagers. The proposal was first tested in one village, Blama, which was relatively inaccessible and had a population of only 120. Because of its isolation it had received little or no medical help from outside. Under the new schemes two nurses from Serabu visited the village once or twice a month, when discussions were held with the health committee. The initial results were encouraging; for example rubbish pits were dug and fenced, attendance at hospital clinics increased and the people were learning a great deal about prevention. As a result the project was extended to three villages at the end of 1976.

A valuable feature of this project is that extremely good baseline data was collected and this is followed up by annual physical examinations of every resident member of the three villages. A register of births and deaths is kept by the clerk of each committee, attendances at meetings are recorded, the committee's knowledge of the topics in the teaching programme are tested annually, spot checks are made of sanitary facilities and so forth. Objectives were set at the beginning of the programme, such as 'A 25% decrease in both the infant and child mortality rates over the first five years, January 1977–December 1981', and more specifically '75% possession of valid child-welfare clinic cards having full immunization coverage'. The six years' evaluation by Dr Ross is still in progress, but by all accounts the targets seem to have been substantially met. There is, for example, no neo-natal tetanus, whereas previously it accounted for 24 per cent of all prenatal mortality.

The Serabu project is a good example of what can be achieved when the potential of village resources is exploited. It is remarkable how many constructive innovations have been suggested by the villagers themselves. For example, the traditional birth attendants, when instructed by the Serabu staff, were quick to learn about the causes of tetanus. It was they who suggested a means of stamping it out by including tetanus vaccination within the ritual process of a girl's puberty rites. At all times the Serabu staff have been willing to listen to the views of the villagers and this has led to a fruitful exchange of ideas. They have learnt to respect strongly held feelings, for example the taboo on men hearing any discussions about pregnancy or delivery; male members therefore withdraw from committee meetings when these topics are discussed.

The initial initiative it is true came not from the villages but from outside. This was so in the Kasa project, and is generally the situation. It can therefore be said that it was the change agency that introduced public participation. The people responded, but to what extent does their continued effectiveness depend on the constant encouragement and support of the Serabu staff? Would all the benefits be lost if hospital staff no longer visited the villages? How permanent are the changes in behaviour patterns that have occurred? For this project it is too early to say, and there is no intention in the foreseeable future of support being withdrawn. All that can be said is that it has shown what can be done at very low cost to create not only better health standards, but a sense of hope amongst the people that they can have a much greater control over their conditions.

Community participation and state policy in health

Health is an area where community participation can be seen to be essential if real progress is to be made. Because the fear of sickness and death is ever present, people are more willing to become involved than they are in matters which appear to them to be less urgent. But just because of these fears strong traditional beliefs surround death and disease, and these have to be understood. Taboos must be respected, behaviour patterns cannot be changed overnight. The people themselves have to learn to accept different ways of thinking and the consequences of this acceptance on other areas of the society must be appreciated. In the field of medicine it is particularly hard for doctors and nurses trained in modern medical schools not to condemn many of the practices they find. But if they are to obtain community support they must learn to be tolerant, and to understand the problems faced by the people themselves. For example, in criticizing lack of hygiene they must understand the constraints under which many people live; unless they are prepared to improve the water supply they must exercise due constraint in what they prescribe (Hardiman, 1984).

The questions raised in this chapter can be examined under several headings.

Who participates?

The Kasa project illustrated the importance of distinguishing between involving only the leaders and the participation of the wider community. Inevitably the initial contact usually has to be made with the existing leaders, as was seen in the Sierra Leone example. The programme was built on the hierarchical structure, first seeking the co-operation of the paramount chief and the section chiefs before approaching town chiefs or village heads. But wider participation was sought at an early stage by various strategies. Central to this was the formation of a village health committee chosen by the community, including all the traditional midwives, and other individuals to look after different aspects of health, such as water, sanitation, medicines and records. The committee included 'a woman with healthy children of her own', who was younger than the traditional midwives.

An active village committee is a crucial element in securing wider participation, as is also demonstrated by the Jamkhed project (Arole, 1975). But even this may not be enough, as decision making and executive action may fall into the hands of a small and self-perpetuating clique, which may act in its own interests with disregard to the wider community. As factionalism is a common feature of communities this is a difficult problem to solve and it may be a case where personnel serving the communities from outside have to hold the balance. They must get to know all sections of society and exercise constant vigilance to ensure that as many as possible can take an active part in improving health both for themselves and the wider society. This leads to the second question.

What does participation involve?

It is a myth to assume that everybody wants to be actively involved in decision-making, or even in the hard work of implementation. The majority of people are usually content to accept the decisions and actions of others so long as their interests are served. Moreover, in the field of health there are many technical matters that depend on professional expertise. Oral rehydration therapy, one of the greatest life-saving methods available, was invented and developed by the medical profession, as were many of the other simple techniques to save child deaths (Grant, 1983). Lay people expect doctors and nurses to possess skills to help them prevent and cure disease even after they have become convinced that many aspects of health care lie in their own hands. Rifkin (1983) cites an example of a community health programme where as it developed the medical professionals, with the assistance of the community development workers, tried to shift into a new role as 'enablers' and 'change agents'. However major resistance to this change came from the community, who wanted the medical staff to remain in the clinic and provide services. In other words, the people themselves felt more confident in their new community development roles, which meant that the medical personnel could fall back into their traditional service roles.

So even if the value of participation is agreed there are different approaches to how it operates. Rifkin (1983) distinguishes between three:

1. The medical approach
This is based on the medical model of health care and the view that health is essentially the absence of disease, and that this can best be done by the application of medical technology. It sees the community in a rather passive role, as following the orders of professionals. It stresses the importance of understanding, on both sides, and expects that the community through this will improve their environment and habits.

2. The health planning approach
This is based on the view that health is essentially the result of the appropriate delivery of health services. All community members should have access, whatever their financial resources. Medical science alone cannot result in significant and widespread health improvements, they must be integrated into a programme which takes account of the underlying causes of ill health, and this must involve the community.

3. The community development approach
This grows from the tradition of community development. It is more community based than the other two approaches, believing that health improvements do not necessarily start with health service activities but rather from the context of better living conditions, such as improved housing, education, and income. It sees development as a 'bottom–up' rather than a 'top–down' process in which community members begin to take control and responsibility for their own health care.

In the 1970s the community development approach became increasingly popular. However, it ran into difficulties, such as the increasing realization that most communities were not homogeneous, and that matters of health were highly political. Therefore existing inequalities had to be taken into account, which takes us back to the earlier question about 'who participates?' In practice many suggested programmes involving participation use elements from all three approaches. And however committed those organizing a programme are to a community development approach, the practical problems involved usually ensure that medical professionals play a more dominant role.

Does participation mean economic self-sufficiency?

This is a controversial issue on which strong opinions are held. Self-sufficiency is used as a criterion of success in the evaluation of some programmes. It is a reaction to the indiscriminate handing out of food, and drugs, which by themselves may do little to improve health. It is also based on the view that people do not value a service unless they pay for it. Again another aspect of the view is based on the fact that the lessons learnt from small-scale projects cannot be replicated if there has been too great a financial dependence on outside resources.

There are various ways in which greater self-sufficiency is sought. In some cases communities are expected to pay the stipends of their part-time village health workers, or the workers are expected to work for nothing. Curative treatment may be charged, as is done at Jamkhed, and this may cover some of the cost of preventive services. A great deal of the cost of environmental services can be borne by the community if local manpower and womanpower is available and willing.

All these ways of mobilizing community economic resources are legitimate and in poor countries may well be the only way of developing adequate services. But to use the goal of self-sufficiency as the main criterion is not justifiable in view of the gross inequalities of income and access to services. Self-sufficiency is rarely considered in urban areas, except perhaps in squatter settlements. Why, then, should it be deemed necessary for rural people? Bang (1983) and Sen-Gupta (1983) both argue that the acceptance of economic self-sufficiency as a goal leads to losing sight of the primary objective which is to improve the health of the people. 'Self reliance of the people in their own health care should not be the objective of the health activity. The funds necessary for health care have to be generated by the economic programmes' (Bang, 1983, p. 6). Although in principle this is fine, programmes have in the meantime to struggle with lack of resources. Whereas self-sufficiency may not be the ultimate objective, in the short run more contributions may have to be found from the community than justice might suggest.

Government programmes and non-governmental organizations

Most of the successful programmes using community participation as a principal method of operation have been run by non-governmental organizations (NGOs). Governments may pay lip service to the principle, but in practice the implementation of it tends to be weak. There are many reasons for this, quite apart from the usual charges against the bureaucratic machinery. For one thing voluntary organizations' projects are on a smaller scale, so community participation is much easier to achieve. Because of their charitable nature these organizations are more likely to employ dedicated people who are less concerned about the career prospects of their job. Often expatriates are involved, whose careers in any case lie outside the country in which they are working. For them employment of this type may enhance rather than retard their career prospects. If the same could be said for nationals of the country the story might be very different. Only a minority of people can afford or are willing to ignore such considerations.

It is also easier for an NGO to be innovative, to test out small pilot projects. Such projects usually generate great enthusiasm, sometimes to a misleading extent, as the original guinea pigs (in the communities concerned) can perform differently when ideas are incorporated in the normal procedure. However, despite this rather cynical note, small-scale experimental projects do serve a useful purpose by indicating the possibilities that exist. Above all, they usually demonstrate a potential which bureaucrats tend to ignore.

If participatory methods are considered to be an effective way of improving health, then they must be incorporated in government programmes if they are to make a real impact. In so far as NGOs have pioneered the way they should be used as a resource by governments. How this can best be done will vary greatly between countries, a subject that was explored by the ACHAN board when it met in June 1982 (*Link*, 1982). It was hoped that the board might be able to articulate some policy guidelines about the relationship, but it soon became apparent that this was not possible as a result of the very different country experiences.

In some countries governments have already responded to NGOs' activities by adopting their ideas. In India the use of part-time village health workers developed by Shah and the Aroles has led to a government scheme for community health workers (now called village health guides). In Korea, community health programmes run by NGOs led to the government establishing the Korean Health Development Institute, which has taken over the experiments of the NGOs, leaving little for them to do. Whereas in Sri Lanka the impact of NGOs has been limited because of a comprehensive government programme.

An important issue in all these cases is the establishment of a satisfactory system of co-ordination between governments and NGOs. Without this there is a danger of duplication, with such examples as an NGO setting up a family planning clinic almost next door to a government clinic, or working in similar capacities in the same village. Every country should set up a body to review issues related to this relationship, such as the co-ordinating council for all NGOs in Nepal. Moreover this body should be in constant communication with government ministers and officials, so that a real understanding develops of policies and practices on both sides and a strategy for co-operation can be formulated.

What of the future?

This chapter has discussed ways in which community participation has been used as a strategy for improving health. Although the principle of participation is as old as communities themselves, the deliberate use of it by outside agencies is relatively recent. Despite widespread interest, meaningful participation as a policy measure does not cover the majority of populations. As we have seen, there are many problems involved and the principle itself may well have limitations. Participation alone is not a substitute for substantial government inputs in, for example, improving the infrastructure. What is now needed is for larger-scale experiments, initiated as part of an overall national health policy. Only then can the long-term contribution of participatory methods be assessed.

3

Education, schooling and participation

ANTHONY HALL

There has been much dissatisfaction with the inability of education systems in the developing world to meet the ambitious goals set for them. In the post-war period education has been viewed simultaneously by economic planners as a major spur to national growth and by individuals in newly independent countries as the principal means of escape from traditional, poorly-paid agricultural occupations into the modern, urbanized industrial sector. Subsequent disillusionment with conventional education structures as vehicles for economic and social transformation has led to a reassessment of their role within the Third World context and to an examination of alternative methods. This has generally taken the form, on the one hand, of an attempt to generate universal access to basic education and, on the other, of experiments with formal and non-formal institutions in an effort to make instruction more relevant to the needs of poor communities. As with attempts at piecemeal reform in other sectors, educational innovations have invariably embraced the notion of increasing the level of people's participation as a prerequisite for achieving objectives which have eluded the élitist school systems imported from the west during the colonial era.

In many economic sectors lack of investment by the state is frequently cited as a principal cause of poor performance. In the educational field, however, investment targets have been met and even exceeded, forming the largest single item in the budgets of most Third World countries. From 1970 to 1973 the GNP of developing countries rose at an average rate of 6.3 per cent while public expenditure on education grew by 13.6 per cent p.a. (Simmons, 1980, p. 28). This massive investment in formal education, particularly at secondary and tertiary levels, has been fuelled by planners' belief in the formation of human capital as an essential prerequisite for sustained economic growth (Becker, 1964; Harbison, 1973). With the benefit of hindsight it seems that this theory was based on a false analogy with European experience where it was assumed that educational expansion had preceded the industrial revolution rather than vice versa. However, the assumed causal link between education and growth was encouraged by the rise of manpower planning, which forecast acute shortages in middle and higher level technical skills in developing countries. It was claimed that schools, universities and colleges would need to increase their output of trained manpower to meet the demand which would undoubtedly arise as industry and commerce prospered.

During the 1960s and 1970s there was, as Table 3.1 illustrates, a formidable expansion in educational provisions at all levels, and particularly of secondary and higher institutions which grew at 12.7

Table 3.1 Enrolment ratios in selected developing countries: primary, secondary and higher education, 1960 and 1978

| | *Numbers enrolled as a percentage of age group* | | | | | |
| | *Primary* | | *Secondary* | | *Higher* | |
	1960	*1978*	*1960*	*1978*	*1960*	*1978*
Low income LDCs						
Bangladesh	47	72	8	22	1	3
Ethiopia	7	38	1	9	—	—
India	61	79	20	28	3	8
Tanzania	25	70	2	4	—	—
Sri Lanka	95	94	27	52	1	1
Indonesia	71	94	3	16	—	2
Middle income LDCs						
Thailand	83	82	13	28	2	5
Philippines	95	100	26	56	13	24
Colombia	77	100	12	43	2	10
Korea, Rep. of	94	100	27	63	5	10
Brazil	95	88	11	24	2	13
Mexico	80	100	11	39	3	11
Developed Countries	100	100	58	82	16	34

Source: Todaro (1977)

per cent and 14.5 per cent respectively compared with 8 per cent p.a. for primary school enrolment (Todaro, 1977, p. 249). Politicians were only too happy to concur with educational planning priorities since they legitimized a positive response to the huge popular demand for access to formal education from people anxious to escape the poverty of the traditional rural sector. This was, after all, a perfectly rational economic choice given the failure of most economic growth strategies in developing countries to provide incentives for the expansion of small-scale farming and the generation of higher levels of income in the rural sector. A combination of population pressures, encouragement of large-scale, capital-intensive commercial agriculture, and the widespread neglect of small cultivators by government have been major factors in perpetuating the migration of the better educated to urban areas as well as a generalized motivation to acquire the educational 'passport' necessary for better-paid jobs in the modern sector. As Table 3.2 shows, the relative average earnings of people in developing countries vary considerably according to educational attainment, even more so than in the west. Thus, the massive quantitative expansion of formal education has enabled governments to satisfy a number of economic, political and social goals at the same time.

Table 3.2   Ratio of average annual earnings by educational level

Country group	Relative earnings Secondary/Primary	Higher/Primary
USA, Canada, Great Britain	1.4	2.4
Malaysia, Ghana, S. Korea, Kenya, Uganda, Nigeria, India	2.4	6.4

Source: Todaro (1977)

It might have been possible in early post-independence days for governments to deceive themselves that they were pursuing the most appropriate educational strategy by concentrating on secondary and higher education, combined with locally relevant targets such as universal primary education and literacy for all. Upward social mobility was possible for a few lucky graduates as posts in government administration were vacated by the departure of colonial powers. Yet once this small number of jobs was taken and industry failed to grow as fast as had been anticipated by the economic planners, mobility was blocked and opportunities became increasingly rare (Foster and Clignet, 1966). Far from education actively stimulating the growth of job opportunities, as the human capital theorists had suggested, unemployment was the order of the day. Levels of educated unemployment rose significantly throughout the 1960s and 1970s, reaching levels of 15–20 per cent among secondary school and university graduates in countries such as Kenya and Pakistan (Simmons, 1980, p. 33). Competition among graduates has led inexorably to a process of what Dore calls 'qualification inflation' (1976) as the modern sector economies have, except in a few notable cases, been unable to provide enough jobs for the growing army of certificated youth.

The mismatch between educational enrolments and job opportunities has had a differential impact on various social groups. By increasing competition for and the qualification 'price' of jobs, expansion of formal education systems has placed children from lower social classes at an even greater disadvantage. Unless employment opportunities are expanded significantly, the advantages conferred by superior social class and status both within schools and in the job selection process mean that wealthier groups will tend to monopolize the market. Rather than facilitating upward mobility and a redistribution of wealth, expansion of the formal educational structure has merely tended to reinforce the existing social order and the privileges of nascent middle and upper echelons of society (Clignet, 1980). Indeed, observers such as Bowles (1980) assert that the state education system is designed specifically to preserve the prevailing economic and hence the social structure.

In addition to maintaining and even, perhaps, aggravating social divisions, educational expansion has been a major factor responsible for the rapid increase in rural-urban migration. According to Todaro (1977) the decision to migrate is motivated by rational economic expectations concerning employment, and the tendency to migrate is higher amongst the educated due to the high private returns to formal education. Yet the expansion of formal educational facilities beyond the point at which it is economically justifiable has made such expectations increasingly long term and has resulted, as we have seen, in a rapid multiplication of jobless graduates.

Educational policy and community participation

The 1970s saw a concerted effort among educational planners, particularly in the multilateral aid organizations who tend to take a lead role in policy-making, to examine alternative strategies which would avert some of these problems. The formal educational structures had served middle-class, urban élites rather well but had failed to meet the needs of the poor majority in most developing countries. This was formally recognized by the World Bank which categorically stated that formal education had been, for the previous twenty years, irrelevant to the needs of developing countries (1974), and proposed a programme of non-formal and vocational education. In a similar vein, UNESCO put forward the idea of lifelong or basic education involving a combination of formal and non-formal techniques (Faure *et al.*, 1972). To the extent that these proposals envisaged extending both academic and vocationally-oriented education and training to those who had hitherto been denied access to the formal system beyond the most elementary stages, they were participatory. The state clearly had a vested interest in creating a less imperfect match between skills taught and existing job opportunities, in reducing the rural–urban migratory flow and the consequent strain on city resources, in cutting down the numbers of educated unemployed and the political threat which they might pose and in increasing overall industrial and agricultural production. However, during the early 1970s, the notion of participation remained implicit, limited to an increase in the number and proportions of populations actually taking part in new programmes.

By the beginning of the present decade this situation had begun to change and there was a realization of the limitations inherent in this model. The new concept of basic human needs (BHN) education (World Bank, 1980b; Noor, 1981) attempts to integrate the previously separate formal and non-formal systems. Rather than attempting to persuade poorer groups to alter their aspirations for modern sector jobs, a futile policy which merely encouraged people to totally reject non-formal education as inferior, BHN education seeks to equip citizens with both general and relevant specific skills. Thus, it focuses on teaching communication skills and general knowledge via primary schools and literacy campaigns, life skills such as hygiene, nutrition and family planning, and production skills for self-employment. It is officially viewed as the most cost-effective way of including in the education system those who would otherwise be denied access to the formal education apparatus. It implies a fairly sophisticated level of planning and management to be able to integrate educational activities across the different sectors, and to co-ordinate the wide variety of institutions from village polytechnics to private businesses required to help reach the goal of universal basic education by the year AD 2000.

A further aim of this basic education strategy is to 'increase beneficiaries' participation in articulating their needs and managing their programs' (Noor, 1981, p. i). The more specifically participatory nature of this approach compared with its predecessor is, one imagines, reflected in the proposed enlarged role of community organizations ranging from primary schools to skills training centres. Yet such community initiatives are no novelty. In Africa these ideas date back to the Phelps–Stokes Commission reports of the 1920s whose central tenet was 'to promote the advancement of the community as a whole through improvement of agriculture, the development of native industries, the improvement of health . . .' (quoted by Thompson, 1981, p. 36). The concept of the total integration of school and community to serve local and national development needs was epitomized by Nyerere in *Education for Self-Reliance* (1967). In Africa as a whole, attempts at linking school and community fall into four overlapping categories according to Thompson (1981). These consist of designing more appropriate, environmentally-related curricula; involving the community in running schools; serving the community directly; and, finally, developing the school itself as a part of the wider community.

Among the first attempts to introduce participatory forms of community-linked schooling were those concerned with 'decolonizing' imported western curricula such as the Entebbe mathematics programme, the African science programme and the African social studies programme, designed to make course content more relevant to local needs and involving a move away from traditional, rote-learning to more dynamic teaching methodologies. While valuable in their own right, these new developments have been widely criticized for failing to question the fundamental role of the school and merely reinforcing the current emphasis on competition and selectivity (Thompson, 1981).

At the primary level there has been a number of curriculum

reform programmes, particularly in Africa, which attempt to balance formal education with a community focus. The Kwamsisi community school project in Tanzania, funded by UNESCO and UNICEF, is one of the best known of such experiments and is discussed below as a case study. The Namutamba experiment in Uganda involves fifteen primary schools and has grown from a small curriculum reform scheme for teaching science in rural areas to a wider integration between school and community for the purposes of basic education. The IPAR project in Buea, Cameroon, has designed a methodology for gradually integrating school and community in the process of spreading basic education (Hawes, 1979).

Similar experiences can be cited from various other parts of the world. In the Republic of Korea, the Saemaul or 'New Village' movement's educational programme is based on curricula adapted to community needs. Students engage in community service and in setting up demonstration projects for villagers while the schools themselves serve as cultural and adult education centres for the community. In Nepal an experimental project at Lahachowk has introduced a programme of co-operation among teachers, health and agricultural extension officers to extend educational facilities to all members of the community. At Comilla in Bangladesh the impact is far greater and the well established community development scheme there incorporates an educational programme which forms an integral part of overall rural development plans (UNICEF, 1978).

Some countries have attempted to extend the concept of the community-linked school to secondary institutions, as in Guinea, for example (Thompson, 1981). The Botswana Brigades provide an alternative form of post-primary education and training to conventional forms and attempt to teach skills relevant to rural development and modern-sector requirements related to job availability. Their self-financing capability is dependent upon close links with communities but they are principally training institutions with little local participation as such. The same may be said of the Kenyan village polytechnics, of which there were 170 in 1978. Designed to train primary school leavers in general rural and technical skills, they have tended to receive relatively little local community support (Thompson, 1981). A similarly luke-warm popular response to non-conventional educational institutions has been reported from Tanzania, where the Folk Development Colleges have, according to Thompson (1981), lost their practical focus.

Other types of non-formal education have been expanded significantly since the early 1970s in the general drive to concentrate resources on activities more immediately relevant, in planners' eyes at least, to pressing problems of rural and urban development. As part of the basic education strategy of the past fifteen years or so, in addition to promoting greater links between the community and the school, there has been a significant expansion of agricultural and health extension, adult education and general literacy training. Viewed as an integral part of a redistribution with growth strategy (Chenery *et al.*, 1974) these policies were seen, through cross-sectoral linkages, as essential for improving the health and nutritional status of the poor majority, for increasing overall productivity and real incomes, and for guaranteeing popular participation in policy formulation (Streeten *et al.*, 1981). The World Bank has specifically identified inappropriate, urban-biased formal education systems as a major bottleneck to rural development and the alleviation of poverty in the countryside, and sees non-formal education alternatives as one of the principal avenues of reform (Coombs and Ahmed, 1974).

Agricultural extension has traditionally been dominated by the notion that the easiest way of improving agricultural productivity is to unilaterally inject knowledge on an individual, face-to-face basis using external agents trained in distant colleges. The spread of 'green revolution' technology in particular brought home the fact that extension models were inherently biased towards the so-called 'progressive' or wealthier farmers producing cash crops, while the majority of subsistence farmers was ignored. Little farmer feedback of information was allowed for and messages tended to be top–down, the extension agent supposedly exercising a monopoly over relevant knowledge (Pearse, 1980; Garforth, 1982). This variety of non-formal education was therefore non-participatory by any definition.

The relative failure of new agricultural technology to improve the lot of the mass of poor farmers led to a re-examination of extension techniques during the 1970s and, in line with the basic needs approach, more broadly based, poverty-oriented methods were developed which it was hoped would spread the benefits of non-formal inputs rather more equitably. As espoused by organizations such as the World Bank and the Food and Agricultural Organization this newer approach, which supplements rather than substitutes previous methodologies, emphasizes the use of farmers' groups as more cost-effective and pedagogically more efficient vehicles for the promotion of learning. It entails the use of more non-directive methods and a two-way communication process which focuses on co-operation, joint action and participatory decision-making. The Kenyan Farmers Training Centres and the Taiwan agricultural extension service are two of many examples of this new philosophy being implemented (Garforth, 1982; Roling, 1982; Coombs and Ahmed, 1974). The development of farming systems research is also a clear recognition of the need for more participatory research and extension techniques as a prerequisite for the design of agricultural systems which are acceptable to small farmers and which do not carry with them the negative social consequences of inappropriate methods imported from the developed countries (Norman, 1978; Clayton, 1983).

Another major area in which non-formal education has received a strong impetus is that of health-care. This subject is dealt with in Chapter 2 of this volume, but it is worth reiterating the point here that the adoption of the primary health-care approach in the last decade has paralleled developments in the agricultural extension sphere. They have both been focused on the local community rather than expensive, distant curative or training centres; they both utilize group learning methods; both make widespread use of para-professional staff; both emphasize simple, traditional techniques where relevant and both involve a degree of participation in the sense that the community is encouraged to diagnose and find appropriate solutions for its own problems without depending totally on the 'superior' knowledge of outsiders (Ahmed, 1982; Garforth, 1982).

Finally, adult education and literacy training have also been included in the package of basic education measures intended to bring about the greater participation of citizens in national and local life. In the words of one observer, 'Literacy would act as the bridge between fatalistic passivity and uncomprehending acceptance, which has been thought of as characteristic of rural peoples, and real participation both in promoting and in determining the nature of the social transformation thought to be necessary' (Thompson,

1981, p. 224). Thus, the large-scale mass literacy campaigns of the 1950s and 1960s sought to extend basic reading and writing skills to the whole population, often combined with instruction in hygiene, nutrition and child care. In the heyday of manpower planning, literacy was thought to be a fundamental precondition for economic growth. Anderson (1966) formalized this concept in his theory of the 40 per cent literacy threshold below which the take-off into industrial growth was impossible.

However, such general literacy did not lead to immediate practical benefits or higher incomes and these campaigns were fuelled rather by educators' belief in their intrinsic as opposed to their developmental value. In 1965 UNESCO abandoned its worldwide campaign for the eradication of illiteracy and adopted a more selective policy of promoting functional literacy for specific target groups, usually on a work-oriented basis. While the debate about the precise relationship between literacy and development continues, most recent thinking suggests that such training should be more systematically linked with other forms of adult education. Paradoxically, the value of the mass literacy campaign both for sustaining overall development and as a basic human right, in spite of the expense and difficulties of implementation, has seen something of a revival recently (Noor, 1981).

Participation in practice

In order to illustrate briefly how community participation ideas have been implemented in the field of education, two case studies have been selected for discussion. The first is the renowned Kwamsisi community-linked schooling project in Tanzania, while the second is the less well known community-organized bench schools of Cartagena in Colombia.

The Kwamsisi community school project

The Kwamsisi community school project, located in North-East Tanzania, was set up with the assistance of UNESCO and UNICEF as part of the country's nation-wide plans for integrating school and community education. Its main aims, Hawes (1979) notes, are to develop literacy and numeracy, self-reliance, equality and the skills and values necessary for life in the *ujamaa* village. Several basic ideas underlie this experiment, the first of its kind and perhaps the best known in Africa. The school is viewed as an integral part of the community and shares with the village a responsibility for developing rural areas. The village development committee and five separate specialized committees include as members both schoolteachers and pupils. Learning patterns and curriculum content are expressly geared to perceived local development needs. Development activities such as agricultural projects, the carpentry workshop and functional literacy are seen as complementary to each other, with local craftsmen teaching their skills in school and the teacher promoting adult education in the wider community.

Kwamsisi has been viewed by the Tanzanian government and by many educational planners generally as an important innovation which could provide valuable lessons for the future. The community school or 'community learning centre' is, Hawes (1979, p. 169) observes, 'being rapidly replicated throughout Tanzania'. Yet serious doubts must be raised as to how far it can achieve its stated objectives. In addition to the experimental curriculum the basic subjects of English, maths, Swahili and political education are maintained and it is these which are examined to determine selection for further education. Thompson (1981) notes that in community schools the number of hours devoted to these examination subjects has been reduced from 40 to 27 to allow for practical activities, thereby placing pupils in these institutions at a disadvantage when compared with non-participants. One independent study of Kwamsisi noted that parents still perceived the community school as a major avenue of upward social mobility for their children and out of subsistence farming, and that half of those leaving the school had either secured or were qualifying themselves to obtain jobs in the modern sector (Bacchus, 1982).

Thus, the 'examination backwash' effect in Tanzania is bound to undermine the credibility and feasibility of community schools. The continued central importance of selection by academic examination, despite official claims to the contrary, will inevitably lead to such experiments being labelled in the popular mind as inferior options which do little to enhance the life chances of their pupils in the competition for improved livelihoods and better paid jobs. To the extent, therefore, that this educational strategy is encouraged against the wishes of the rural community and in pursuit of the political philosophy of the state, as expressed by Nyerere in *Education for Self-Reliance* (1967), the Kwamsisi model appears to fall squarely into the category of 'manipulative participation'.

The Colombian bench schools

The Colombian bench schools are an example of a much rarer breed of educational project. These do not form part of a predetermined government strategy imposed on the populace, as in the Tanzanian case but, rather like the Kenyan *harambee* schools, represent the poor community's spontaneous response to the inadequacy of state educational facilities. An official survey revealed the presence of thirty-two such schools in the city of Cartagena on Colombia's Atlantic coast. They have been set up by poor slum-dwellers for children aged 4–7 years to prepare for entry to primary school by teaching literacy and numeracy, and also to make it easier for mothers to take up paid employment outside the home. Classes are held either in people's houses or in the open air, and each pupil brings his/her own pencil, notebook and wooden bench. The teachers are usually mothers with five years primary schooling and are paid a fee of one dollar per month per pupil.

The Office for Slum Rehabilitation of the Colombian government and UNICEF initiated a support programme to provide the community schools with improved facilities and teacher training. The International Education Laboratory (LIDE) has developed educational kits designed to stimulate the children's intellectual development and creativity. Initial results have, according to UNICEF (1978) been encouraging and widespread parental participation has been observed. Furthermore, interest has spread from schooling to other community concerns such as road repairs, youth clubs, hygiene and recreational activities. The success of the Colombian bench schools thus illustrates the importance of respecting the community's priorities. Community-linked participatory education is possible as long as the expressed wishes of those affected are respected and official assistance is provided within those parameters set by the people themselves. To the extent that these conditions are met, the Colombian case suggests that a degree of authentic participation at local level may be realizable.

Community participation, education and the state

The above discussion has so far focused on ways in which governments and international organizations have sought to use participatory education methods as a way of reaching a larger section of the population than is possible via the conventional school and college structure. Not only was this viewed as a means of alleviating pressure on the increasingly overburdened formal education system whose graduates could not, generally speaking, be absorbed by the limited modern sectors in the developing world. Non-formal education could also, it was believed, make instruction more relevant to community and national developmental needs at large. Two birds could be killed with one stone. An additional bonus to this approach was that it went beyond narrow economic objectives and enabled the state to increase the degree of active popular participation in the process of transformation. At least, this has been the rhetoric of the basic human needs philosophy with regard to the education sector.

The experiences revealed here suggest that what participation has occurred has been of the incremental and, occasionally, of the manipulative type. Considering firstly the community schools movement discussed above, it seems evident that this has not been seriously adopted as national policy in the vast majority of cases, but has been limited to a handful of pilot schemes dependent on external funding and expatriate personnel without whose support they would collapse (Bude, 1984). Governments have not on the whole been willing to make the financial commitment necessary to guarantee the long term independence and viability of such schemes. Furthermore, as Thompson points out (1981), due to the heavily centralized nature of planning, few of these innovative projects actively involve local communities in design and management activities. In some cases, also, government involvement goes beyond simple *laissez-faire* incrementalism but uses the community school network for political propaganda purposes. This kind of manipulative participation is well illustrated by the system of political education in Tanzanian schools where, according to Hirji, the curriculum is 'dominated by sloganeering and sycophancy, the emphasis being on forms, appearances and declarations rather than scientific understanding of social reality' (quoted by Thompson, 1981, p. 270).

Virtually the whole of the non-formal education movement can be viewed as a form of 'imposed participation'. Its insignificant impact in the total education picture is due to a number of factors including limited finance and personnel. However, the most important reason is perhaps a generalized rejection by the very people that non-formal education is intended to serve. The masses had certainly not been consulted when foreign experts designed the concept and exported it to the Third World. What officials saw as a more appropriate package of measures better suited to the needs of rural populations, the people themselves saw as an inferior form of instruction which would not equip them for the modern sector jobs they so desperately desired. What governments perceived as an approach which would reduce the pressure on cities and urban higher education facilities by keeping more people in the countryside, rural dwellers perceived as a two-tier system of educational apartheid which would reinforce class barriers even further and deny to them forever a chance of breaking the vicious circle of poverty. Even countries such as China and Cuba which have undertaken structural reforms to equalize income distribution, to improve the livelihoods of the rural population and alter the pattern of job opportunities, have experienced considerable difficulty in persuading students of the benefits of such non-formal approaches as ruralized or vocationally oriented curricula.

In Cuba, for example, Dore (1976) notes that although income differentials have been reduced and there is no longer so much prestige attached to non-manual work, owing to the adoption of school learn-and-work and other programmes, students are still motivated primarily, and their performance assessed, by competitive examinations. He reaches a similar conclusion in the case of Tanzania where, despite widespread curriculum reform and the new roles defined for primary and secondary schools in the countryside, élitism predominates and 'examination marks remain the major criterion for success' (Dore, 1976, p. 119). China attempted to sever the links between formal educational qualifications and career opportunities during the cultural revolution. Unger (1980) describes how the government tried to radically alter the formal education system which favoured pupils from better educated families by allocating them to jobs regardless of academic performance. In this sense the Chinese attempt to modify the formal structure in order to discourage élitism can be viewed as more participatory since, in theory at least, it should have allowed more opportunities to those from less educationally privileged backgrounds. At the same time, the emphasis on practical skills should have made pupils more receptive to industrial career opportunities. Yet the system proved unworkable because students lost their motivation to study once competitive examinations were abolished, nor were they prepared to accept being drafted into low-status occupations.

Despite offical enthusiasm in many countries for educational reform and the introduction of non-formal techniques over the past two decades, there is much popular resistance to changing the system. Those that have a choice still prefer to take their chances within the highly competitive and selective formal education system. People's perception is that, even within the context of limited job markets, the traditional school structure still offers the best opportunity of escaping poverty. This view is certainly borne out by economic studies which point firmly to the high financial returns to secondary and higher education for the individual, given the heavy rates of government subsidy involved. The resulting mass political pressure on governments to provide such educational facilities means that, generally speaking, 'it is the private rather than the social rate of return that drives the system forward' (Blaug, 1972, p. 170).

Non-formal community education is treated with considerable suspicion by its intended beneficiaries because, quite simply, it is seen as reinforcing a dual system which reduces further still educational opportunities for the children of poor families. Superficially it allows greater access to more 'appropriate' forms of instruction for a larger cross section of the population and thus generates more participation. This is the view which educational planners would wish Third World populations to internalize and be content with. However, the populations of developing nations are not so easily fobbed off and their definition of participation is rather different. For them, participation means one thing only and that is gaining access to well-paid, modern sector jobs and decent living conditions. Formal education is the means of entry into this wider world. As Martin observes, '*They* have no cosy ideas about the idyllic self-contained rural village. They know that unless they can gain access to, and understand, the institutions and forces that impinge on their world they will be denied the chance to participate fully in society' (1982, p. 6). The strength of parental determination that their children shall progress up the educational ladder is illustrated by the Kenyan *harambee* schools established by local communities in parallel with and closely modelled on the government school system (Thompson, 1981). The case study of the Colombian bench schools also illustrates the same point. When given the opportunity of participating in and designing the education structure, therefore, the community opts not for non-formal community-linked education but for conventional instruction.

The lesson from this experience is clear. No matter what new educational strategies are devised, and regardless of any built-in notions of participation, they will fail miserably unless the wider structure of opportunities is also changed. The various non-formal alternatives discussed above will not gain popular acceptance unless a direct link is established between adoption of new educational methods and subsequent improvements in people's incomes and livelihoods. Thus, ruralized curricula will only be of use to the community if other reforms are introduced which will make small-scale farming viable and profitable. Depending on circumstances, measures could range from improving people's access to land and complementary inputs such as seeds, fertilizers and credit to changes in agricultural pricing policy, which often works against small farmers, in order to subsidize food prices for politically more important urban consumers. Yet the priorities for economic development chosen by most Third World governments have been based on industrialization and the development of modern, capital-intensive agricultural sectors, resulting in the relative neglect of small farmers and their needs. Only a handful of countries, both Socialist and non-Socialist, has chosen a path based on strengthening the small-farmer sector. Nations such as Taiwan, China, Japan and Korea have opted for what Pearse (1980) calls a 'peasant-based' strategy involving extensive land reform along with institutional and political support for the small farmer as a complement to industrial expansion. Where the structure of opportunities and economic incentives has been substantially modified to make commitment to non-formal education a rational personal choice which will bring substantial benefits to the poor, educational innovations stand a much greater chance of success.

It is difficult to avoid the conclusion that the concept of participation embodied in the basic needs/non-formal strategy of education is of dubious validity. The numerous educational innovations designed to bring more appropriate forms of instruction and training, particularly to rural populations, have met with little success. Most governments have acceded to the pressure of popular aspirations and expanded the formal system well beyond the level at which it could be economically justified, paying lip service to the notion of non-formal education by permitting a limited number of externally funded pilot schemes. A generous interpretation of such moves would label them as incremental participation, a piecemeal attempt by well-intentioned planners to reduce pressure on the formal structure. In other cases intentions are more clearly manipulative and non-formal education is inextricably tied up with political indoctrination.

Perhaps not surprisingly, the underprivileged majority has decided that the most authentic form of participation is the freedom to compete within the existing élitist system. Either implicitly or explicitly, as in the case of the Kenyan *harambee* schools, they reject the imposed participation of the basic needs strategy which suggests that they should be content with a 'second best' type of education. On this basis, government attempts to expand the role of non-formal alternatives are doomed to failure unless, as already mentioned, they are matched by job opportunities. There may be some scope for encouraging greater community involvement in the design and management of special programmes through measures such as decentralized planning. On balance, however, this will not detract from the fundamental scepticism with which non-formal education is popularly received. In the long run, therefore, it may be that the only way of making schooling more genuinely participatory is to generate the economic growth and the life chances which will enable an expanded formal educational system to function in a more egalitarian fashion.

4

Community participation and rural development

ANTHONY HALL

The last few decades have witnessed rapid increases in rates of economic growth in many developing countries. The benefits of this progress have, however, tended to be concentrated within urban upper and middle income groups as well as the rural élite of traditional landowners and newer commercial farmers. The mass of poorer cultivators and their families have, by and large, not been able to share significantly in the fruits of national expansion. The problem of rural poverty continues to be a pervasive one and as insurmountable an obstacle to balanced growth as ever. The World Bank has estimated, for example, that about 85 per cent (550 million people) of those living in absolute poverty (defined as an annual income of less than US $50) reside in rural areas. Some 75 per cent of this total is concentrated in Asia, particularly in India, Bangladesh, Indonesia and Pakistan. In Africa large numbers of rural poor are to be found in Ethiopia, Sudan and Tanzania. Latin America, which is more heavily urbanized than other continents, accounts for only 4 per cent of the rural absolute poor (World Bank, 1975b). In sub-Saharan Africa up to 95 per cent of the population lives in the countryside, most with an annual income of under US $100 (Lele, 1975). The extended drought and associated problems experienced in recent years have no doubt substantially increased rural poverty levels in this area. Generally speaking, urban and rural income differentials are large, with average city earnings in some countries being up to nine times those in the countryside (Lipton, 1977).

Apart from levels of absolute poverty and marked income differences, other social indicators reveal the gross disparity in living standards common to most developing countries. Rural areas are provided with poor health and educational facilities, as well as inadequate domestic water and electricity supplies. Partly as a direct result of this lack of government investment in basic services, but also due to the general neglect of small farmer agriculture, social problems are more evident in rural areas. These include higher rates of malnutrition, illiteracy and ill-health which are reflected in lower life expectancy rates. Table 4.1 shows that life expectancy is significantly lower in poorer countries, which are predominantly rural, and higher in middle-income nations which are characterized by high rates of urbanization. For example, Mali and Malawi with rural populations of 88 per cent and 94 per cent respectively have among the lowest life expectancy rates, while Brazil, Mexico and Argentina, which are all around 50 per cent urbanized, have the highest life expectancy figures.

The precise extent of rural poverty is often difficult to ascertain for several reasons. Firstly, published global and national poverty statistics do not usually distinguish between urban and rural areas except at the most general level. This may be partly for political reasons, that is, a reluctance on the part of governments to admit

Table 4.1   Life expectancy in selected developing countries

	Life expectancy at birth (in years, 1981)
Low-income countries	
Bangladesh	48
India	52
Mali	45
Malawi	44
Sierra Leone	47
Angola	42
Middle-income countries	
Brazil	64
Mexico	66
Argentina	71
Costa Rica	73
Dominican Republic	62
Hong Kong	75

Source: World Bank (1983)

their inability to deal with the problem. Other explanations are to be found in the methodological problems of collecting accurate data on incomes and other social indicators in countries which are ill-equipped for this purpose. A second and related factor behind what one suspects could well be an underestimation of the true extent of rural poverty lies in what Chambers has called its 'unperceived' nature (1980). That is, the poorest communities are often the most isolated, their members illiterate, having little contact with the world of officialdom and the least likely to join associations such as co-operatives or rural syndicates. Professionals working in rural development programmes also do little to break down these barriers of communication, tending to be urban and middle-class oriented who prefer to issue commands and travel in style rather than attempting to empathize with their clients, the rural poor, to listen sympathetically to what they have to say or to get mud on their boots.

As mentioned previously, many developing countries have experienced significant rates of economic growth in recent years. From 1965 to 1982, for example, their average rate of increase in gross domestic product ranged from 2–8 per cent (World Bank, 1983), higher even than for industrial countries. However, the greatest proportionate increase has been in manufacturing and commerce. Growth in agricultural output has remained stagnant and thus declined as a percentage of GNP. Figures in Table 4.2 show that although agriculture accounts for most employment in developing countries, it contributes a much smaller proportion of GNP. As Todaro notes, 'This is in marked contrast to the historical experience of advanced countries where agricultural output in their

Table 4.2   Output and employment in Third World agriculture

Third World regions	% of labour force in agriculture	Output of agriculture, forestry and fishing as % of GNP
South Asia	71	25
East Asia	55	20
Latin America	40	25
Africa	65	40

Source: Todaro (1977)

early stages of growth always contributed at least as much to total output as the share of the labour force engaged in these activities' (1977, p. 222). The same author observes that from 1950 to 1970 per capita food and agricultural production in the Third World increased by a mere 1 per cent. Performance was particularly bad during the 1960s and, in Africa during this period, both agricultural and food production actually declined, suggesting a 10 per cent decrease in food consumption for Africans in that decade (Todaro, 1977, p. 223).

State policies and rural development

A combination of factors has been responsible for these trends including demographic pressure as well as natural disasters such as the extended drought and famine in sub-Saharan Africa. However, the major reason behind the generally poor performance of the agricultural sector is to be found in the types of economic growth strategy pursued by developing countries in the post-war period. Throughout the 1950s and 1960s the commonly held view was that industrialization held the key to rapid economic progress and that agriculture was relatively unimportant in promoting growth. The theories of western economists such as Rosenstein-Rodan (1943), Lewis (1955) and Rostow (1960) did much towards legitimizing this belief in capital-intensive industrialization under a free market capitalist system, combined with heavy infrastructural investments. Yet this choice seems to have ignored historical evidence from the west where the expansion of industry in both Europe and the USA was accompanied by substantial growth in the agricultural sector, both to supply the burgeoning towns and cities with basic food items as well as to create large new markets for manufactured goods in the countryside as farmers' incomes grew. During the 1950s and 1960s, for example, in eighteen selected developing countries, agriculture received only 12 per cent of total national investment but contributed 30 per cent of GNP and provided over 60 per cent of total employment (Todaro, 1977). It is also a well-known fact, documented by the World Bank (1982) amongst others, that in many countries short-term political expediency has taken precedence over long-term development. Prices paid to agricultural producers and, hence, rural incomes have often been kept artificially low by governments anxious to maintain the support of politically important urban populations through favourable food prices.

One of the reasons for the relative neglect of agriculture in this period was the widespread belief among planners and policy-makers that traditional values held by small farmers were an insurmountable obstacle to the introduction of the 'modern' entrepreneurial ethic deemed essential for economic advancement. Thus, poor farmers were seen not as victims of their own situations and limited resource bases, including negative government policies, but as inherently conservative, fatalistic and resistant to change. This attitude began to alter in the mid-1960s with the publication of new ideas which saw the peasant in a somewhat different light. The small cultivator was now viewed as an essentially efficient and economically rational producer who generally made the best use of the resources at his disposal. He could not achieve more because he lacked the technological means and the price incentives to do so (Schultz, 1964). The food deficits of the 1960s combined with this new belief in the economic potential of the peasantry led to a policy of promoting production through massive technological inputs and commercialization of agriculture which has continued largely unmodified to the present day.

Perhaps the best-known manifestation of this strategy is the so-called 'green revolution' which sought to bring about rapid increases in agricultural production and incomes for all types of farmer. The introduction of hybrid seed varieties of wheat, corn and rice was thus in theory 'scale neutral', offering the opportunity for small farmers to progress. Yet the experience of the past two decades has cast serious doubt upon the ability of technological solutions to improve the livelihoods of poor farmers without accompanying agrarian reforms and controls on the ways in which government policies are implemented. Although food production has been increased and nations like India transformed from rice importers to exporters, the 'green revolution' has at the same time generated much poverty and inequity. Many authors such as Pearse (1980) and Griffin (1974) have shown how larger landowners have been able to monopolize the complementary inputs such as irrigation, fertilizers, insecticides, credit and agricultural extension facilities which are essential to success in this enterprise. The most successful or 'progressive' farmers have thus been able to expand their landholdings at the expense of the less commercially able, generating landlessness and rural unemployment, and increasing the flow of migrants to the cities.

Belated attempts have been made to correct these imbalances through specific policies such as the World Bank's 'poverty-oriented' approach (1975), an initiative which was closely followed by other western governments in their aid programmes (Hall, forthcoming). These changes are reflected in World Bank lending figures which show that from 1961 to 1965 almost 77 per cent of bank credit was for electric power or transportation and only 6 per cent for agriculture. By 1981 a full 31 per cent went to agriculture and rural development, about half going to poverty-oriented projects (Ayres, 1983). This policy was closely related to others put forward during the 1970s which stressed the importance of directing benefits to the poorer sectors rather than expecting the fruits of development to automatically 'trickle down' to the masses. These included the 'redistribution with growth' ideas of Chenery and others (1974) and the basic human needs philosophy proposed by the ILO in 1976 (Streeten *et al.*, 1981).

An integral part of these new policies was the notion of increasing the level of people's participation in development activities. It was noted that in the past planning had been highly centralized and bureaucratized, encouraged by the use of systems analysis imported from the west as well as the frequently authoritarian or paternalistic attitudes of planners and policy-makers. The failure of many schemes was attributed to a lack of popular participation by beneficiaries in implementation and evaluation, causing severe management problems (Rondinelli, 1983). Another observer concluded that 'Projects appear almost always to have originated to fulfil purposes of regional or national élites and the bureaucratic imperatives that result' (Gran, 1983). Many have taken an essentially pragmatic view of the importance of participation, arguing that it is 'a necessary condition for rural people to manage their affairs, control their environment and enhance their own well-being' (Gow and VanSant, 1983, p. 427). Some development planners, however, have embraced the concept as a kind of magical 'missing ingredient' from development packages which, once provided, would guarantee success irrespective of other considerations such as the structural, administrative and political preconditions necessary in order for participation to function.

However, the participation ideal has been almost universally adopted by the major multilateral development aid bodies, as well as several bilateral institutions. The principle UN agencies have all taken up participation including the ILO, FAO, WHO, UNESCO and IFAD. One body, UNRISD, has set up a major research programme into the concept and implementation of participation (Pearse and Stiefel, 1981). In 1977, shortly after launching the basic human needs approach, the ILO introduced its PORP (Participatory Organizations of the Rural Poor) programme. The fundamental role of participation in the BHN strategy has also been highlighted by Streeten, *et al.* (1981). The FAO has initiated its own people's participation programme (PPP) in rural development, while IFAD has also stressed the importance of the concept in the design and administration of credit schemes for poor farmers in the Third World (1983). Rather less conventionally, Haque *et al.* (1977) put forward the concept of 'Another Development' which stresses the non-quantifiable dimensions of development and a closing of the 'consciousness gap' between the leaders of society and the masses.

Community participation and rural development

Community participation may be broadly divided into that which is carried out under the auspices of the state and that which remains relatively free from government control. As we have seen, there has been a clear increase in state commitment to the idea of promoting participation as one way of making the process of guided development more efficient. This has become particularly noticeable within the last decade but even before then, participation ideals were encouraged through initiatives such as the community development, *animation rurale* and co-operative movements. Community development and *animation rurale* were instigated in British and French colonies respectively both before and after independence to assist rural reconstruction and nation-building. The idea became popular amongst governments as a convenient, politically neutral strategy for mobilizing the rural population. Community development workers and *animateurs* would 'awaken' the peasantry from its supposed apathy and indifference towards progress. As this concept was transferred from Africa to the Indian sub-continent as well as to other parts of Asia and Latin America throughout the 1950s and 1960s, the theory was that governments and rural populations would unquestioningly pool resources, united in the common purpose of promoting overall economic growth.

Yet the history of these two movements illustrates the fairly narrow limits within which the state is prepared to define and accept the notion of community or popular participation. Despite their democratic overtones community development, and particularly *animation rurale* with its strong tradition of central direction under French administration, soon became vehicles for implementing pre-established official programmes which allowed participants little real say in decision-making. The strong pressures from central government 'transformed the village-level worker from a coordinator into a salesman for line-ministry programmes' (Gow and VanSant, 1983, p. 429). The very concept of a unified community was questionable as social divisions became apparent and the consequent unequal distribution of benefits increased conflict and friction in the countryside. India's community development programme did not give the people a collective voice but, on the contrary, 'encouraged the process of atomization and discouraged the formation of people's organizations' (Gaikwad, 1981, p. 331). Similarly, in post-revolutionary Mexico the government's community development initiatives are perceived as a means of imposing the values of village-level workers on others and as an attempt to 'buy off discontent with concessions which do not tackle the underlying causes of backwardness and poverty' (Cosio, 1981, p. 350).

In socialist states also, true participatory ideals appear to be relatively short-lived and rapidly give way to mechanisms which are designed to impose controls on the rural population rather than allow involvement in decision-making. Following the Arusha Declaration of 1967 Tanzania took significant steps to institute participatory procedures for development which included state control of the major means of production, collectivization into *ujamaa* villages and administrative decentralization. However, after 1972 it appears that these original ideals were scrapped, and, according to Mushi, 'the participatory functions of the people's organizations at the grass-roots level were given peripheral attention' (1981, p. 238). Participation and 'political awareness' became equated, in the eyes of the Tanzanian State, with acquiescence to official policy directives. In pragmatic terms the result was a high rate of project failure attributed in large part to the increasingly authoritarian management structure which allowed little time 'to the peasants and local leaders to do feasibility studies or to evaluate their own successes or failures and draw appropriate lessons' (Mushi, 1981, pp. 239–40). A similar pattern may be observed with regard to the Ethiopian peasant associations, considered below as a case study.

Rural co-operatives were also considered to be an ideal channel for promoting popular participation. Based on the western concept, the establishment of official co-operatives proceeded rapidly throughout the 1950s and 1960s alongside the community development movement. They were seen as a politically neutral form of mass organization which would allow members to exercise control over production and the distribution of benefits. However, the notion of political neutrality was shown to be illusory as co-operatives were used by the state to promote top–down procedures and policies and extend control over rural areas. These organizations have also, on the whole, tended to be undemocratic internally, dominated by wealthier producers able to control both decision-making and access to subsidized government inputs such as credit and technical assistance (UNRISD, 1975). Even within the pioneering Comilla community development project in Bangladesh, new co-operatives created specifically to assist poor farmers were soon 'dominated by the rich farmer–money-lender–trader class' while the pressing problems of poorer producers were ignored (Haque *et al.*, 1977, p. 93). Thus, institutions ostensibly created to increase participation by and flow of benefits to the poor may end up by marginalizing them even further as relative poverty levels increase.

A second major and increasingly important category of community development is that undertaken independently of the state through non-government organizations (NGOs). This approach to increasing people's participation in development is discussed in greater detail in the final section of this chapter. In order to illustrate some of the major differences between the state and non-government strategies, two case studies will now be considered.

The first examines the Ethiopian peasant associations, while the second looks at the movement of fisherwomen in the Brazilian North-East.

Ethiopian peasant associations

The 1974 socialist revolution in Ethiopia initiated radical changes in society which gave the rural poor widespread hope of being able to participate more effectively in the development process than they had been able to in the past. A feudal mode of agrarian production together with peripheral capitalist farming had, prior to the revolution, marginalized and impoverished the peasantry. In the south of the country in particular the state had dispossessed the peasantry of its land and redistributed property to the local nobility and nascent urban élites, leaving only about 6 per cent of land grants for the landless and unemployed (Abate and Teklu, 1982). Exploitative obligations to landlords further increased inequalities while government agricultural policies favoured larger-scale cash crop farming for urban consumption and for export, thereby encouraging mechanization, the polarization of landownership, increasing landlessness and pauperization of already poor cultivators.

Following the revolution a land reform was proclaimed in 1975 and peasant associations (PAs) were formed on the basis of the traditional village unit. PAs were empowered to redistribute expropriated lands, establish co-operatives, encourage local infra-structural development and villagization. In order to speed up this process the government deployed 60,000 urban-based students and state functionaries, known as *Zemecha*, to teach the principles of Ethiopian socialism, to discourage 'individualistic' tendencies and to assist in the formation of the PAs. In the space of only four years over 28,000 associations with a total membership of 7.3 million households were formed (Abate and Teklu, 1982).

In common with other revolutionary Socialist regimes such as China and Cuba, Ethiopia has attempted a rapid mobilization of the population in order to undertake radical reform and initiate a process of rapid economic transformation. Thus, 'the concept of greater peasant participation emerged as a cornerstone of the revolutionary process' (Oakley and Marsden, 1984, p. 55). Yet this whole strategy is very much geared towards fulfilling the predetermined goals of the state. The peasantry itself, for example, had no say in the nature and content of the post-1974 agrarian reforms, which had already been decided upon. In the initial reform stages, furthermore, the *Zemecha* remained in control of the peasant associations and allowed the peasantry only a nominal participation in their administration (Oakley and Marsden, 1984). Examples have been cited of these outside agents attempting to impose the concept of collective farming on the PAs, an idea which has met with relatively little enthusiasm from the peasants themselves. In recent years also there has been a high rate of absenteeism, reflecting a dwindling interest on the part of poor farmers in their associations, due perhaps to their limited effectiveness in bringing improvements and acting as a channel for effective mass participation.

Using the classification outlined in Chapter 1, therefore, the Ethiopian peasant associations seem to fall squarely into the category of manipulative participation. Within this particular context, participation signifies involvement of the people only in terms of their contributing labour and resources as well as making a firm commitment to the state's political ideology. It has little to do with freedom of decision-making or the encouragement of independent initiatives by autonomous groups. To the extent that mass mobilization for nation-building and conformity with national policy objectives are the major state priorities as in the Ethiopian case, the concept of participation is bound to be rather a narrow one.

Brazilian fisherwomen

The following case study is representative of an increasingly large number of small-scale development initiatives supported not by the State but by private organizations, frequently with the aid of foreign NGO funding. It involves a group of some 100 fisherwomen in a small coastal area of North-East Brazil. Caught in a vicious circle of poverty, low productivity and under-capitalization, their opportunities have been further limited by the fact that their interests are not represented in the government-controlled fishing co-operatives (*colonias*).

In 1975 a diocesan community worker made contact with one or two women and started a process of dialogue. As the group grew in size the fisherwomen were able to analyse their own basic problems, which they defined as those of powerlessness and the lack of any effective organization. The fisherwomen eventually decided to attempt a solution to their problem by improving their participation in and influence upon the fishing *colonias*. Notwithstanding the problems of operationalizing what are essentially non-quantifiable dimensions of development (Oakley and Winder, 1981), observers noted that over a five year period there were substantive behavioural changes within the fisherwomen's group away from characteristics of apathy, fatalism and paternalism and towards those of group solidarity, organization and commitment to common goals. In more concrete terms, the fisherwomen initiated a movement to acquire the individual legal documentation necessary for registration with the *colonia* and to be able to gain voting rights. This concerted action culminated in the election of two of the group's members to the board of the co-operative in 1981 in order to represent the interests of the women for the first time (Oakley and Marsden, 1984).

This example stands in total contrast to that of the Ethiopian peasant associations discussed above. The project did not form part of a preconceived strategy with predetermined objectives. These were only decided upon after a period of several years of group discussion and self-examination by the women involved in accordance with their own interests as they themselves defined those interests. Unlike the Ethiopian *Zemecha* the Brazilian community worker did not arrive with the intention of forcing community members to follow one particular path or line of thought but rather to encourage the participants to think for themselves and instil within them the confidence to take concerted action along the lines they considered most appropriate to their circumstances. Far from being manipulative, therefore, the Brazilian fisherwomen's project is probably as near to the ideal of authentic participation as is possible in practice.

The state, rural development and community participation

At various stages in the design of rural development strategy governments have sought to include the notion of popular participation. Yet because of the increasingly dominant role of the state in directing change and the need to combine this with political mobilization for the purposes of national integration, there must be limits to the extent to which authentic participation can be permitted. As has been shown in the case study of the Brazilian fisherwomen, authentic participation (as defined also in Chapter 1) signifies allowing freedom of decision-making and control over internal activities to those taking part in the development process. Governments with a firm commitment to pursuing certain macro-economic and social goals cannot, therefore, allow the kind of popular involvement in policy-making which might challenge the legitimacy of these overall objectives. The practice of participation in this context will thus necessarily be either of the *laissez-faire* incrementalist kind or of the more consciously manipulative type.

In a sense, therefore, state-directed participation is a contradiction in terms. This is because the nature of popular involvement becomes so limited as to virtually defy use of the term 'participation'. In effect the concept becomes purely instrumental, useful to government for making the pursuit of pre-established goals more efficient. Thus, many so-called 'participatory' programmes do not go beyond taking advantage of local cheap labour for construction of public works or, for example, involve token consultations with village chiefs in order to gain the acquiescence of the population. Other programmes are more consciously dictatorial and make little attempt to conceal their true objectives. The cases of the Ethiopian peasant associations discussed above, the Chinese rural communes and the Tanzanian *ujamaa* policy, really leave little room for doubting what most if not all governments understand by participation. It is useful only as long as it serves to help achieve national economic and political objectives but it is not valued as an end in itself. In other words, 'Participation seems to mean getting people to do what outsiders think is good for them' (Heyer *et al.*, 1981, p. 5).

Development planning is still overwhelmingly characterized by what has come to be known as the 'blueprint approach' which allows no effective popular participation. The responsibility for taking the initiative in determining what form development should take rests firmly in the hands of central planners. Local people are consulted only in so far as such contacts allow the preconceived strategy to be finely tuned and made more efficient on the ground, along the instrumentalist lines already discussed. The rural population is the subordinate partner in this arrangement, occasionally allowed to voice an opinion but who must not protest too vehemently. Despite widespread use of the language of participation in many development plans it has been argued that 'the rural poor do not as yet have any direct part to play in rural development projects' (Oakley and Marsden, 1984, p. 65). Yet the dilemma experienced by policy-makers in attempting to reconcile participation with the need for centralized planning is a very real one which has been recognized by the World Bank: 'The manner in which early participation is to be achieved and balanced with the need for overall guidance and control from the centre, is a problem which can only be resolved within each country' (1975, p. 37).

Although the ideal of authentic participation is probably not possible under state direction, nevertheless there are ways in which the degree of popular involvement in the planning and implementation of rural development could be increased. One suggestion concerns the adoption of a 'process' approach to planning, in contrast to the 'blueprint' style which has been predominant until now. The process approach rejects the assumption that projects are simply vehicles for the application of predetermined government solutions to developmental problems, but is based instead on a process of continuous dialogue between planners and beneficiaries in the search for the most appropriate strategy (Gow and VanSant, 1983). This style also implies what Chambers (1983) calls 'reversals in learning' in which outsiders learn from farmers and the rural poor. A variety of techniques are put forward, ranging from sitting, asking and listening to joint research and development as tools which could 'encourage and enable those being trained or educated to learn from the many below and not just from the few above' (p. 209).

Yet these exhortations remain somewhat idealistic. It is almost unheard of for the rural poor to be effectively consulted by government planners. Furthermore, once established most rural development schemes are characterized by authoritarian, hierarchical management structures which allow little or no beneficiary participation or information feedback. Hall (1978) found this to be the case on official irrigation projects in North-East Brazil where farmers are obliged to follow management directives unquestioningly. An exception to this rule is the National Irrigation Administration in the Philippines which since 1976 has developed

Community participation and rural development

a participatory style that has resulted in the creation of strong irrigator's associations (Bagadion and Korten, 1985; Chambers, 1983). Another example is the PIDER programme in Mexico which, according to Cernea (1983), recognized the need for farmer participation particularly at the initial planning stage and throughout the project as a basic prerequisite for long-term success. This principle is also being extended to social forestry schemes where beneficiary participation in social analysis is seen as essential for obtaining grass-roots support (Cernea, 1981).

Another suggestion for improving the level of popular participation in government programmes is to decentralize certain powers and functions in order to increase local control. This refers not just to transferring command over some aspects of policy and resource allocation, but also to changes in the ways in which bureaucracies operate to permit more local autonomy. These 'reversals in management' (Chambers, 1983) could, however, be difficult to implement if the government has little control over rural areas or if powerful line ministries exist which strongly oppose such challenges to their authority. The state could make resources available to local organizations through revenue-sharing or block-grant arrangements in order that they might undertake their own development activities. Yet the monopolistic power of local élites may easily subvert such participatory moves unless the state takes firmer action to redirect resources to the neediest groups.

These suggestions assume that only the state has the power to initiate moves in the direction of greater popular participation. However, poor farmers may themselves take steps to increase their own control over events and thus circumvent the government's frequently manipulatory policies, whether these are labelled 'participatory' or otherwise. Barnett (1981), for example, has described how farmers on the Gezira scheme in the Sudan divert irrigation water from cotton fields, against official instructions, to assist their own food crops. In his study of government irrigation projects in the semi-arid North-Eastern interior of Brazil, Hall (1978) noted several tactics employed by hard-pressed small farmers to avoid the rigid controls imposed upon them by management, which included the illicit marketing of a substantial proportion of total production. Official reactions to such peasant resistance tend not to be in the direction of greater understanding and dialogue, but the imposition of further controls and restrictions.

101

Official strategy, whether promoted by individual governments or by multilateral agencies such as the World Bank, tend to assume that the rural population is totally incapable of initiating a process of rural development. Yet experience has clearly shown that, given the right conditions and incentives, the rural masses do indeed have the enterprise necessary to plan and execute a range of development activities in furtherance of their own interests. Here, of course, lies the crux of the matter. These interests are frequently at odds with those of the state so that such independent initiative is generally frowned upon or even suppressed. Coulson (1981) has described the case of the Ruvuma Development Association in Tanzania, one of the original models for the later official *ujamaa* policy, yet which became so successful that it was banned as a threat to government authority. The farmers of Jamaane in Senegal took the initiative of forming a peasant association and hired an agronomist to advise them, but they clashed with the irrigation development authority which had other plans for their future (Adams, 1981).

Given the limitations on the possibility of achieving any degree of authentic participation under state tutelage, perhaps the only channel for pursuing this objective lies outside of direct government influence via non-government organizations. Many NGOs have a firm commitment to challenging the socio-economic structures which underlie poverty and exploitation. NGO-backed projects range in size from individual community schemes with a handful of participants, to middle-range activities such as the Brazilian fisherwomen's project and even regional organizations embracing thousands such as the Bhoomi Sena (Land Army) Movement of Maharashtra State, India (de Silva *et al.*, 1982). Whereas schemes supported by voluntary agencies are generally considered to be marginal to the mainstream of rural development, in practice their impact is far greater. The ratio of government to non-government assistance, for example, is only about 6:1 (Lissner, 1977).

This type of rural development is far more likely than state-guided initiatives to lead to a process of authentic participation. Perhaps the main reason for this is that, whereas official policies tend to be predicated on the assumption that peasants are incapable of defining their own development path, non-government projects start from the opposite premise that only the beneficiaries themselves know what is the most appropriate course of action. The

Community participation and rural development

contrast in approach is also reflected in the choice of working methods. The top–down management techniques of the 'blueprint' approach are firmly eschewed in favour of dialogue, mutual consultation at all stages, self-reliance, collective action to solve group problems, democratic decision-making and local control over project activities. If they are well enough organized such bodies or movements may become powerful pressure groups, a source of countervailing power which can challenge government authority when this is felt to be against the best interests of the people. This philosophy contrasts so strongly with official techniques that Galjart (1981a) has gone so far as to label it 'counterdevelopment'.

It would be oversimplistic, however, to suggest that, on the basis of the above analysis, all state-directed rural development should automatically be rejected as manipulative and all unofficial interventions welcomed as the only genuinely participatory vehicle for promoting the welfare of the rural poor. It must be borne in mind that NGO supported schemes often have their own drawbacks. A frequently heard criticism is that such projects tend to be small and geographically dispersed, and are difficult to multiply on a national scale. Indeed, this feature is virtually a precondition for authentic participation. Once projects grow in size beyond a certain point the problems of bureaucratization and growing official links with government increase the danger that they could lose many of their original 'participatory' features such as dialogue and democratic decision-making (Galjart, 1981b).

Other criticisms relate to the methodology used to establish and promote small-scale development projects. Many voluntary organizations use 'conscientization' techniques which assume that the poor have an incomplete or imperfect perception of their own reality and that their 'awareness' must be heightened as the basis for group action (Freire, 1972; Oakley and Marsden, 1984). Yet this is in many ways a patronizing view which, as Berger has pointed out in no uncertain terms, presupposes that 'lower class people do not understand their own situation, that they are in need of enlightenment on the matter, and that this service can be provided by selected higher-class individuals' (1977, pp. 137–8). This perpetuates what Berger calls a 'hierarchical view of consciousness' in which outsiders are deemed to be the best judges of poor people's perceptions.

Conversely, of course, outsiders can easily fall into the trap of assuming a much greater degree of spontaneous solidarity than is actually the case, simply by projecting their own politicized values on to the poor and underestimating potential sources of village conflict. Whatever the assumptions, there is always the danger that community 'animators' or 'facilitators' will, consciously or otherwise, adopt a manipulative role and decrease the villagers' own freedom of choice in a non-participatory direction. It must also be said that, no matter how well-meaning the external funding agency, the mere fact of financial dependence on outsiders makes the notion of true community autonomy somewhat spurious. While the imposition of certain funding criteria and procedural requirements may be justified on the grounds of increased administrative efficiency or in terms of responsibility to the donating public, these do often place limitations on the scope of project activities and serve to emphasize what is fundamentally a power relationship between the givers and the receivers.

On balance, then, it is difficult to avoid the conclusion that the participatory mode of rural development, as defined in Chapter 1, is far more difficult to achieve through official channels than via non-government means. Yet it has to be recognized that, with all their apparent advantages, the impact of voluntary organizations will be limited comparatively speaking due to financial and logistical problems. It is doubtful, in fact, whether most rural communities would even desire to assume complete responsibility for promoting development. In order to reach greater numbers of rural poor there is therefore a strong case to be made for increasing state participation in rural development. At the same time, however, this should be designed so as to allow for much greater beneficiary involvement in preliminary decision-making as well as project execution than has been the case to date. The means exist for combining government resource allocation with local initiatives and community control over the development process. What is needed is a political commitment to adopt these methods on a wide enough scale to transform the rhetoric of participation into concrete action.

5

Urban development, housing and community involvement

DHANPAUL NARINE

Community participation in urban development provides an effective platform for the poor to influence the decision-making process. In the United States the concept of 'maximum feasible participation' became fashionable in the early 1960s. The overall objective of this policy was to create avenues whereby the views of urban neighbourhoods could be taken into account in planning services for the cities. In developing countries, community power as a dynamic approach to urban development brings into focus complex political systems and the manner in which they are interpreted to facilitate accommodation. While there appears to be little consensus as to how the process of accommodation is to be achieved, any analysis which questions the capacity for accommodation is likely to reveal variables which are common to the political systems of both the industrial and developing world. A salient factor which emerges is that centralization and bureaucratic control are unable to satisfy effectively existing needs for the majority of people in both worlds. It is largely this inability that creates viable conditions for community participation. In developing countries the urban landscape is ensconced between hope and despair. Rapid population increase, unemployment, the proliferation of slums and squatter settlements, poor health and sanitation have all contributed to a distorted image of urban areas. In an effort to explain poverty, connotations such as apathy, deviance and malaise have been attributed to the poor. Lewis's (1966) typology of the 'culture of poverty' is significant in that the blame for poverty is placed firmly at the door of the less privileged. Portes (1971) writing on life in the Chilean slums attacks the poor for being 'vagabonds and delinquents' and sees life in the slums as being 'a refuge of ultimate destitution'. The tendency to type-cast urban poverty in negative labels ignores the spirit of activism which is prevalent among the poor and which is central to their achievement of social mobility. The use of mechanisms, especially information housing, have reinforced communal solidarity and at the same time led to improvements in levels of living. This chapter expands on the activism of the urban poor. It will begin by looking briefly at urban trends in developing countries. The conventional response to the housing question will then be discussed after which two case studies will be presented to highlight the impact of community participation on the urban planning process.

Urban trends and urban problems in the third world

The populations of developing countries are moving into its cities at unprecedented rates. By the end of the twentieth century it is estimated that the world's population will exceed 6 billion persons, of which over 80 per cent will live in the developing world. A breakdown of urban growth rates in different world regions is shown in Table 5.1. It is generally agreed that the growth rates in the developing countries have more than doubled those in the industrial developed countries. Such increases are seen as being consistent with the process of modernization (Lerner, 1967). Demographic analyses show that in developing countries the rates of natural increase are far greater than those of the developed countries. The reasons for such increases are often interwoven into

Table 5.1   Urban growth rates in the Third World, 1950–80

Region	Average annual growth rate (%)		
	1950–60	*1960–70*	*1970–80*
Africa	4.4	4.8	5.0
Asia	4.5	3.4	3.5
Latin America	4.5	4.2	3.9
Third World	4.5	3.9	4.0

Source: Todaro (1979)

complex domestic social arrangements. Where fertility is enmeshed with the prevailing culture, as it invariably is, a high premium is usually placed on pronatality. In such cases attempts to control population are unlikely to have great success.

High fertility rates have a direct impact on urban growth in developing countries. Despite variation in individual countries it is generally agreed that migration and natural increase are the main contributors to urban increase. In dealing with migration, Brown (1974, p. 108) points out that 'The continuous and swelling flow of people from countryside to city is creating a serious social crisis, the ramifications of which will eventually affect the quality of life among much of mankind.'

This social crisis, it is believed, is due to a multiplicity of factors. The 'decay' of the environment leading to crime and deviance is a popular viewpoint (Clinard, 1966). Rural decomposition and the penetration of capitalism on the institutions of the society are also linked to the impact of urbanization (Castells, 1977; Roberts, 1978). While King (1976) sees the problems of the urban areas as being essentially a colonial hangover, Lipton (1977) suggests that the neglect of the rural sector, in favour of urban development, creates imbalances in the distribution of services. The theories relating to the urban crisis are by no means exhaustive. In reality, the pressure on urban social services, alienation and the rapid growth of slums are all symptoms of the striking poverty which beset developing countries.

The literature is replete with lurid descriptions of the urban poor in the Third World. Lewis (1966), as has been seen, dwelt on the pathology of the poor by underplaying their capacity for action. It is apposite to note that researchers who worked in the same cultural zone as Lewis found that the urban poor were actively participating in community projects which heightened cohesion and alleviated poverty (Safa, 1974; Mangin, 1970). The relative nature of poverty and inequality continued to invite differing interpretations. Quijano (1974), for instance, equated poverty with the marginalization of society in a generalized manner while Roberts (1978) approached the issue from the point of view of a lack of basic services. These include access to adequate employment and housing. The concept of unemployment as an indicator of urban poverty can be misleading. While there is a tendency to attribute the unemployment situation to heavy in-migration to the urban areas, it should be emphasized that many migrants find jobs within a short period. These may include labourers, messengers, vendors and domestics and other unskilled occupations. Attempts to link urban poverty and inequality to underemployment is also questionable. The informal sector in developing countries is quite dynamic in providing employment to the urban poor. Despite criticisms that the informal sector promotes capitalism (Moser, 1979) the informal sector is well entrenched and offers opportunities for the poor. The National Development Plan of Botswana (1976–81) admits to the important role being played by the informal sector as an employer and proposed measures to integrate this sector into the mainstream of the economy in an effort to end hostility between the two sectors.

Population increase in the urban areas has placed tremendous pressures on the existing social services. The shortage and in some cases the inability of these services to deal effectively with the problems of the poor have led to the institutionalization of stereotypes. Migrants are generally associated with crime, deviance and alienation. This line of reasoning has firm foundations in western social science. Wirth (1938) drew attention to the 'anomic' behaviour which existed in the American cities. In addition, the biases of scholars who found city life appalling were reflected in their writings. Attempts to transport the notion that the urban areas are the main centres of criminal behaviour has to be treated with caution. In developing countries support institutions are particularly active in the urban areas. They serve as important networks to cushion the feelings of alienation by reactivating cultural norms and in some cases even act as channels for employment. Clearly these institutions provide the buffer which is needed for migrant adaptation (Little, 1972; Lloyd, 1979).

The provision of adequate housing to the urban poor remains one of the main problems facing both planners and politicians in the cities of developing countries. The United Nations (1974) estimates that more than one third of the population in the cities of developing countries live in slums (Table 5.2 shows the proportion of population living in slums in selected cities). The *bustees* of India, the *favelas* of Rio and the *bidonvilles* of Morocco are often seen as interminable blots on the urban landscape. Inadequate sanitation, overcrowding and poor health facilities provide ample ammunition to those who see slum settlements as comprising the 'dregs of

Urban development, housing and community involvement

Table 5.2 Proportion of the population of Third World cities living in slums

Third World city	Year	Proportion living in slums (%)
Amman	1974	12
Bangkok	1970	15
Bombay	1971	45
Brasilia	1970	41
Calcutta	1971	67
Caracas	1974	40
Colombo	1972	44
Dacca	1973	18
Dar-es-Salaam	1970	50
Delhi	1971	36
Guatemala City	1971	30
Ibadan	1971	75
Jakarta	1972	26
Karachi	1971	23
Kuala Lumpur	1971	37
Lima	1970	40
Manila	1972	35
Mexico City	1970	46
Nairobi	1970	33
Panama City	1970	17
Santiago	1973	17
Seoul	1970	30

Source: United Nations (1974), Drakakis-Smith (1981)

humanity'. This conclusion quite aptly questions the interpretation of housing as an agent of social change. From the earliest times shelter was linked to happiness and safety. The United Nations (1962) saw housing as being more than a series of buildings. It recommended that housing should be seen as a link between an individual and his community. In 1974 the United Nations in the World Housing Survey again stressed the social attributes of housing. The Latin American Report (1975), however, links shelter to the total environment. It states that:

Giving a family shelter is very little (sic) if there is no running water, if the head of the family is unemployed or does not have the means to reach his place of work, if the housewife cannot obtain her basic article in the neighbourhood, or if her children have no school to attend. Furthermore it is not enough to secure material needs if the air is not fit to be breathed, if concrete has advanced over green spaces, if beaches, rivers and lakes have become dumping grounds for urban civilisation. (Latin American Report, 1975).

Shelter in this case refers to the quality of life rather than the mere physical habitation of a given urban area. In its general sense then the interchangeable use of 'shelter' with 'dwelling' and 'housing' does not negate the fact that the quality of life index is paramount when discussing the housing needs of the urban poor.

In evaluating the housing conditions in developing countries indicators such as overcrowding and occupancy have been used. The most well known of these indicators is the existence of slums and squatter settlements. However, the use of indicators can be misleading since they do not necessarily imply poor housing standards. In dealing with official housing norms Turner (1976) argues that the housing problem has arisen because planners and politicians have created standards which they cannot match. They have failed to see slum housing from the viewpoint of the dweller; the latter through participation improves over time his own dwelling. In addition, the emphasis placed on standards may be totally unrelated to the local environment. Singapore represents a good example of a country where the use of western standards resulted in neighbourhood and community centres being underused (Yeh, 1975).

Urban development, housing and state policies

In an effort to solve what the state regards as the urban problem, various approaches have been adopted. The evolution and application of these policy approaches have been influenced by a great variety of factors including the adoption of western models of urban planning and housing, the degree of professionalization in urban development, centralization and the perceptions of political élites of the seriousness of urban problems and threat of poverty.

Urban planning is one of the most popular policy measures

adopted by Third World governments in their attempts to deal with urban problems. Introduced originally by European colonial rulers, urban planning procedures have been extended to cover many cities in the developing countries. Vast sums of money have been spent on preparing master plans which would, it was hoped, produce a well structured pattern of urban growth. Foreign consultancy firms were widely used to prepare these plans and to assist in their implementation. But, in spite of the enormous effort that has been expended, urban planning has not lived up to the expectations of politicians, bureaucrats and professionals. Rapid urban growth has rendered plans obsolete even before they were completed, and confounded those who believed that urban planning would transform the cities of the developing countries into well designed and orderly places.

Urban planning has not only failed to take account of demographic realities but has been insensitive to social conditions in the urban areas. An architectural and engineering bias in the planning process has emphasized infrastructure at the expense of human needs and has been naively unaware of the nature and extent of urban poverty. Failure to take account of the poverty problem, which is so characteristically evident in Third World cities, has often reduced planning to a paper exercise. Insensitivity to human needs has extended also to the way governments have formulated housing policies. Indeed, there is a good deal of evidence to show that state urban housing policies have been brutal in their effects.

One example of the way the state brings its weight to bear on slum and squatter communities is to employ a policy of clearance and demolition. The use of the bulldozer is usually accompanied by the belief that the erasure of the 'urban eyesores' is a solution to the housing problem. The use of force is common in the demolition of slum and squatter settlements in Third World countries. There are vivid examples in the housing literature of the mass demolition of so-called slums in Africa, Asia and Latin America. Recently, the world's attention has been focused on the efforts of the South African government to evict squatters from communities such as Crossroads near Cape Town.

Where clearance is linked to urban renewal programmes, displaced populations are not always rehoused and where they are, they may not find the new housing suitable. The point is that such schemes are seldom motivated out of concern for the poor; frequently, they are used for prestige projects with the aim that they would become national showpieces. It is generally agreed that slum clearance and demolition as an approach to deal with housing for the urban poor is not that which is likely to produce positive results. According to Turner (1969, p. 525), 'The basic problem of slums is not how to eradicate them but how to make them liveable.'

The role of the state as a builder of housing for the poor has also been far from successful. In many developing countries, symbolic housing schemes tend to have little relevance to local needs (Dwyer, 1975). The use of western standards and designs and materials often result in housing for the poor being alien to the local environment. The failure of planners fully to appreciate how space is perceived and organized by and among the poor has resulted in mis-investment. In addition, high rise buildings often provide no more than uncomfortable boxes which trap the initiative of the poor. These elevated shacks are often abandoned resulting in the return of the poor to the slums. Apart from relevance, a key factor in the provision of public housing is that it is usually out of range of low income earners. Hence it is quite common for middle and upper income groups to purchase rights of occupancy from the poor.

Brutality in state housing policies is to be found also in some of the other measures that have been adopted by Third World governments in their attempts to deal with urban problems. A good example is the use of urban control policy. The overall objective of such a policy is to limit migration to urban areas, which it is claimed, is the cause of overcrowding, the growth of slums and pressures on existing urban facilities.

One country, in which these control measures have been clear and specific, is South Africa. Black people are not allowed to live in the urban areas unless they have permanent jobs. A period of fifteen years residence in the urban areas is no guarantee that the authorities will allow the family of Black migrants to join them in the cities. While the policy of apartheid seeks to ensure that the cities remain free from Black settlement, Black families continue to go to the towns in search of employment even though they risk imprisonment and deportation to the rural areas. The reaction of the authorities in demolishing the migrants' squatter settlements has not deterred migration. In Indonesia, a decree passed in 1970 sought to limit migration into Jakarta. But this experiment was not successful as regulations became difficult to enforce (Simmons, 1978). The action by the Kampuchean government in 1975 of clearing out the cities appeared to have aimed at overt political control rather than rural development. A country in which rural development is linked to control measures is China. Migration control is enforced rigidly and special permits are required in order for villagers to travel to the cities. But China's urban control policies have been linked to substantial investments in rural areas and a concerted attempt to raise rural levels of living. Tanzania, influenced by the Chinese example, attempted to introduce spatial policies aimed at population redistribution with little success.

Urban control policies have made little impact on restricting movement and promoting urban development. These measures are often implemented at great social costs producing embittered relations between sections of the community. Conventional housing policies have often had the same effect. In addition, there is little evidence to show that these policies have resulted in an improvement in the quality of life for the poor. The problems of overcrowding, traffic congestion, poor sanitation and inadequate housing continue to be familiar sights in the 'urban sprawl' of developing countries.

Although it would be factually incorrect to depict all state urban development policy as insensitive and brutal, there is little ground for claiming that conventional policy measures have brought significant improvements in the social conditions of urban areas. Indeed, there is a good deal of pessimism in urban development circles about the prospects of the poor under conventional state policies. It is for this reason that far more emphasis is today being placed on a people-centred approach which stresses the need for community participation in urban development and urban housing.

Urban policy and community participation

Although there are numerous variations on the community participation in urban development theme, most writers on the subject believe in the mutual co-operation of government and local community to improve urban conditions. This two-way process means that governments should be able to recognize the potential of the urban poor as innovators. In other words, governments must capitalize on the activism of the poor if co-operation with popular action as a strategy is to be effective. Since governments are enablers and providers of resources, official support for urban projects involving community participation is likely to demonstrate the growing need for recognition which local projects require.

These ideas have been advocated for many years but it is only in comparatively recent times that they have been widely applied, particularly in the field of urban housing. During the 1950s and 1960s, for example, United Nations advisers such as Abrams and Koenigsberger attached great importance to the active involvement of ordinary people in urban renewal projects. Drawing on his experience of the United States, Abrams (1964) reported that self-help housing projects among the poor could bring about better housing conditions. But, as he cautioned in a later publication (1966), self-help housing programmes must be properly planned and managed if they are to be successful. Koenigsberger *et al.* (1980) in their treatment of slums and squatter settlements also attested to the virtues of community action. They recommended, for instance, that a series of action programmes be drawn up in dealing with urban development problems in Singapore. Urban renewal has to be linked to the community for it to be realistic. From his experience in India, Clinard (1966) reached a similar conclusion arguing that the mobilization of local communities and their effective involvement through the use of community development methods could help to deal effectively with the problems of urban slums in Third World cities.

However, these advocates of community involvement did not succeed in substantially modifying existing policy approaches which continued to stress centralization, professionalism and bureaucracy in urban planning and housing. But, as it became more and more apparent that conventional measures were making litle if any impact, it was recognized that new ideas were urgently needed. Community participation has now become a central issue in urban development and particularly in the provision of urban housing. Its elevation and acceptance owes much to the ideas of Turner and Mangin whose experience of slum communities in Latin America led them to formulate a coherent strategy for popular participation in slum improvement schemes. They concluded that the inhabitants of the slums were eager to escape abject poverty and improve their environment. Representations made to the authorities resulted in the provision of basic services and significant changes in local conditions. As Mangin (1970) showed, concessions granted by the authorities were largely secured through effective community participation.

The contributions of Mangin and Turner have paved the way for community participation in urban development and housing to be taken seriously by both the political and planning establishment. Turner, in particular, has advocated the virtues of self-help housing. His writings have transcended the slums of Lima; the application of the self-help principle has firmly embedded itself in housing theory. A recurrent theme in Turner's writings and indeed one which has formed the cornerstone of his approach is the idea that housing should be seen not as a noun but as a verb. According to Turner (1980, p. 204), 'What matters mostly about housing is what it does for people, not what it is materially.' But, as Turner maintained, self-help housing can only be effective if it involves security of tenure and dweller control. People will only invest their time, effort and resources to improve their own housing conditions if they are secure in the knowledge that they have permanent rights to residence. Dweller control, through which people can decide what type of house to build, should be invested in the individual. Such control automatically leads to dweller satisfaction. When the building of a house is the responsibility of individuals, they are more likely to put up with its imperfections. Housing 'by the masses' in which there is participation, is much more viable than 'mass housing' in which there is overt government control.

Although popular, Turner's position has been subjected to criticism from various sources. Drakakis-Smith (1981) took the view that the application of Turner's ideas may lead to a neglect of the private sector. Dwyer (1975) posited that self-help housing can legitimize slums and squatter settlements, thereby leading to inferior housing. Burgess (1979), writing from a Marxist position, argued that Turner's proposals represent a capitalist con-trick designed to perpetuate the class system. Swan (1980) was critical of Burgess's position and suggested that it is through the use of self-help housing and community participation in urban development that the poor are able to improve their living conditions. In addition, it is doubtful whether a transition from capitalism to socialism 'will magically solve the housing problem' (Hardiman and Midgley, 1982, p. 236).

The writings of Abrams, Koenigsberger and Mangin and Turner on the role of participation in urban housing infiltrated and influenced policy decisions both at the United Nations and the World Bank. In 1975 the United Nations Economic and Social Council proposed that popular participation should be adopted as a national development strategy. In the following year (1976) the United Nations Habitat conference in Vancouver was more explicit about the role of public participation in relation to housing. The Conference recommended that:

> Public participation should be an indispensable element in human settlements, especially in planning strategies and in their formulation, implementation and management; it should influence all levels of government in the decision-making process to further the political, social and economic growth of human settlements. (United Nations, 1976b, p. 73).

The World Bank, impressed by the participation of the poor in building their own housing, launched a 'direct attack' on poverty through the use of the basic needs approach. The World Bank (1972) financed sites-and-services schemes with the emphasis being placed on owner-built construction. It is estimated that the Bank has assisted 'community sponsored' projects to the tune of US $3500 million through 1982, with an average of 62,000 households benefiting from the project for the year 1981/82 (Williams, 1984).

Community participation in low income housing having been adopted by international agencies permeated and gained acceptance by national governments in developing countries. In India, at the state level, community participation enabled the construction of houses and, equally important, the building of communities (Shah, 1984). In other parts of the developing world projects promoting the ideals of participation are active in tapping the productive resources of the poor. The 'freedom to build' project in the Philippines, and the Building Together Company in Thailand are indicative of this trend. In addition, FUNDASAL in El Salvador is one of the largest non-governmental housing agencies and is the only one of its kind to be aided by the World Bank. This agency promotes community organization and uses low income housing as its principal instrument.

Although the principle of community participation in urban development and urban housing is now much more widely

accepted in intellectual circles and among officials at the international agencies, it is not the case that the ideals of community
participation have been universally applied throughout the
developing world or that they have been properly and effectively
implemented. Nor are they uncontroversial.

Resistance to the involvement of ordinary people in urban
development remains strong among many planners in the Third
World who, as Hollnsteiner (1977) pointed out, have difficulty in
understanding the views of the masses. The planners are usually
drawn from the middle class and after years of technical training
have difficulty in empathizing with the poor. Civil servants are
likely to regard the involvement of ordinary people in the planning
process as a nuisance and may actively subvert the attempts of local
communities to have a say in the planning process. Politicians often
fear that participation will weaken their authority and in a number
of countries, genuine participatory activities are perceived as being
subversive. This is particularly likely where participation involves
activism. Indeed, government sponsored participatory activities
may well rebound in that once popular awareness is aroused,
people may make militant demands and engage in actions that
threaten the *status quo*. As Hollnsteiner (1977) observed, this may
produce repressive responses from the state. In addition 'the
designation of the legitimacy/non-legitimacy line remains an
ambivalent product of differential outlooks where government and
militant peoples' groups are concerned' (p. 8).

It is for this reason that a number of observers have argued that
community participation in urban development invariably results
in a concerted effort by the state to subvert and manipulate local
people. Gilbert and Ward (1984) are adherents of this point of view
arguing on the basis of studies of three Latin American cities, that
the state effectively uses the mechanisms of community participation
as a means of social control. They found that in each of the three
cities, the state has been 'successful in deflecting opposition by
making concessions, by providing services, by co-opting leaders or,
in the last resort, through repression' (p. 239).

These issues will be examined again later in this chapter but first
to illustrate how community participation ideals have been applied
in the field of urban development and housing, two case studies
have been selected for discussion. The first comes from Africa and
deals with a community housing project which utilized self-help

principles. The second, which comes from India, describes an urban renewal project in which an attempt was made to mobilize slum dwellers to participate not only in the improvement of their homes but the local urban environment as well.

The Chawama self-help housing project, Kafue, Zambia

The Chawama self-help housing project in Kafue, Zambia was undertaken jointly by the American Friends Service Committee (AFSC), the Kafue township council and the Zambian government. The purpose of the project was to encourage 228 families to join in constructing houses with a reasonable security of tenure. The first construction group started in January 1970 and by August 1973 most of the houses were built.

The principle of self-help found ready acceptance by the Zambian government. In fact the idea of participation is one which is actively promulgated in Zambia's development plans. The concept of 'participation democracy' in which the decentralization of power is implemented forms an important plank of Zambia's political system. In the field of housing, Zambia's own sites-and-services and squatter upgrading schemes incorporated elements of participation. These included the choice of sites and building materials. In 1967, however, when the government sponsored the aided sites-and-services schemes the response was slow. The practice of self-help did not take off since prospective residents hired their own construction groups. The idea of community participation had not really jelled. The Chawama housing project then was in a position not only to exploit the national commitment towards participation but to study less successful attempts at aided self-help housing.

Kafue situated 26 miles south of Lusaka was chosen as the area for the project in an effort to contain the unprecedented spread of the squatter problem. The input of the AFSC was significant. It contributed 61 per cent of the project total cost and provided the field director and construction supervisor. The recruitment of nine Zambian staff, including community development workers and construction teachers, became the core for in-service training. The training of both the AFSC and Zambian staff emphasized the need for the community participation approach to be adopted as the key element in the project.

In selecting would-be home owners, preference was given to

squatters living in the area. A total of forty-eight families were divided into construction groups; prior to the commencement of construction they participated in study sessions. These sessions dealt with the project plan, the implications, home ownership, the selection of materials, construction methods and so on. A work exchange agreement was signed in which each family pledged a minimum of 1000 hours work to the group.

When actual construction began in January 1970 a conflict of expectations became evident. The staff expected the schedules to be met. Home builders on the other hand became disenchanted when it was evident that the houses of some group members would be completed before the building of other members' houses. In order to ease internal tension, plans had to be revised and in keeping with a group discussion all brickmaking was completed before further construction.

One of the main problems which faced the construction groups was the continued maintenance of morale; members tended to lose motivation once building had commenced. Each group had an internal structure which was related to the larger decision-making body. A group, for instance, had a chairman who through skill and patience was able to resolve problems in the early stages. It should be pointed out that group members were not homogenous, they did not speak the same language nor did they share the same cultural affiliation. A group had direct access to the construction instructor who was on hand to settle work problems and to ensure that building materials were readily available. The community development workers were essential in lifting the morale of workers by convening meetings, resolving conflicts and publicizing the project.

The nine construction groups comprising 140 families found that while their grievances could be heard at the group level, interaction between groups was inadequate. By late 1970 the formation of a group co-ordinating committee resulted in a greater exchange and flow of information between the staff and groups and the groups themselves. The sharing of experience, the giving of advice and support led to greater solidarity. The group co-ordinating committee was in a better position to deal with the personal issues affecting members. For example, when a building group sought help to deal with members who were not 'pulling their weight' the committee recommended counselling instead of expulsion. The committee was also instrumental in advising on matters relating to the ecology of the project for 1972. Kafue residents were cutting down the trees on the hillsides for firewood. This activity was done adjacent to the project site, thus increasing the chances of soil erosion. The committee after discussions with the Kafue township council ruled that no more trees should be cut. The committee also distributed fruit tree seedlings to Chawama residents.

One notable feature of the project was the participation by women. The traditional barriers which formerly limited womens' role in the decision-making process was broken. The fact that women became representatives of construction groups created venues for expression and eventually de-emphasized the distinctions between men's work and women's work.

The Kafue project as is evident was an experiment in community participation and not just a housing construction project. It sought to link housing with the quality of life in the entire community and to foster a sense of communal awareness. The second case study in slum upgrading in Hyedrabad, India, is also notable for this feature.

Urban renewal in Hyderabad, India

The two cities of Hyderabad and Secunderabad in India have witnessed a fast growth rate in population. In 1983, 23 per cent of the population were living in 470 slums; the population was estimated at half a million persons. By any standards this growth in slums was high. In 1981–2 joint co-operation between the housing development corporation (HUDCO) and the municipal corporation representing the state government saw the benefit of the application of a policy of upgrading. The construction of 4300 houses in 34 slum areas was started. A loan of 6000 rupees was to be given to individual families. The requirement was for the beneficiary family to provide 1000 rupees. The average size of a family was seven persons whose average monthly income ranged between 250 and 350 rupees. Slum dwellers worked in a number of jobs. The cottage industries, weaving, carpentry and cobbling were the main areas of occupation. The common factors associated with slum life were highly visible prior to upgrading. Health conditions were poor with ringworm, dysentry and malnutrition being prevalent. The rate of literacy was also low with 74 per cent of the population being unable to read and write. The upgrading of slums while it aimed to provide 'decent and appropriate' houses, saw the provision of these other services as essential for the success of the project.

One interesting factor which emerged from surveys undertaken revealed that the squatters preferred upgrading to the construction of new dwellings. Demolition, in their view, would lead to the loss of control over land and personal belongings. In addition, the dwellers might not get a suitable alternative site, might be charged high interest and be exploited by slum landlords. Once upgrading was agreed upon as the policy to be adopted, community participation became the principal mechanism for the successful completion of the project. The urban community department of the municipal corporation became deeply involved in establishing rapport between families and the political establishment. These officials lived in the slums for long periods in an effort to understand local needs. They also organized and participated in functions which were relevant to the project. These included seminars on the virtues of working together. In a society where caste differences could have undermined the sense of solidarity, organizers arranged cultural programmes to bring the community closer together. In fact 85 per cent of families belonged to the scheduled castes. Such participation had tangible results. The manufacture of local building materials transcended local cleavages. Families whose skills were linked to their caste manufactured materials for the entire community at a much lower price than that of the market. These materials included bricks, doors and window frames. The technical input supplied by the municipal corporation was in a position, therefore, to employ a pool of skilled labour which already existed in the local community. The standardization of plots, agreement in basic designs in keeping with town planning regulations and the grouping of families on the basis of affinities were important elements in the exercise of community participation. Although the basis was laid for a successful completion of the project, it was not all smooth sailing. One of the main problems which the community faced was that of motivation – a tendency not dissimilar in the Kafue project as well. Participation placed an obligation on the community. Land which was provided by the state government could not be used for anything else except the construction of a house. There were also deadlines to be met since construction had to be completed within a given time period. If

121

these conditions were not met then the state government could re-enter and reclaim the site.

The impact of the upgrading programme was felt in the community as a whole. Prior to upgrading, the slums had no access to facilities such as water, sewerage, parks and other community welfare services. As a result of upgrading through the direct efforts of the community, living conditions improved immeasurably. Families constructed their own houses which afforded protection and enhanced security. Internal spatial arrangements also underwent change. Toilets were delinked from multi-purpose rooms, partitions erected and lofts, shelves and grills constructed to add to aesthetic appearance. Water supply and sewerage disposal have improved conditions and the need to carry water has been eliminated, thereby allowing for daily baths.

In the area of health, the incidence of sickness declined significantly. Illness, before the commencement of the project, accounted for the loss of around ten to fifteen man-days a month. As a result of upgrading and improved living conditions, the incidence of illness was reduced to three man-days per month. The construction of schools as part of the upgrading exercise led to an increase in educational awareness among dwellers. The distinction between male and female education was reduced and families were spending as much as 30 rupees per month on their children's education.

There appeared to be improvements in other areas of life as well. Gambling and excessive drinking declined as the responsibility of families increased. In terms of the domestic arrangements a change in the system of cooking led to the observance of more hygienic standards. The use of fuel as a substitute for wood reduced pollution. It also led to the use of metal utensils as opposed to earthen pots. As the social status of residents increased, two distinct changes were observed. Firstly, the consumption of nutritious foods such as milk and green vegetables became common. Secondly, greater attention was given to personal appearance; the sale of clothing increased and families made greater use of footwear.

The impact of the slum upgrading project in Hyderabad was felt both at the area and family levels. At the area level, community facilities were provided. These included water, sewerage and electricity. A community hall with a television set had added to the leisure and income of the settlement since nominal charges are made to view special TV programmes. Special nutrition programmes were established for children and *balwadis* catered for the primary school children. At the family level, titles have been given to the owners of plots. There have been changes in the occupational statuses of dwellers as movement towards permanent jobs became evident. In a study done on three slum communities, it was shown that after upgrading, monthly income increased by an average of 87 per cent. This was due to an increase in the number of earners in most families. The combined effects of security, occupational change and stability of the family have been the main factors accounting for this accelerated pace.

Community participation, state policy and urban development

The two case studies reveal that community participation can and should be a two way process and that state programmes need to be linked to the efforts of local people to improve urban facilities. Where the political will exists and where resources are combined with a determined effort to involve local people in urban development schemes, the poor will respond.

However, the belief that community participation provides rosy solutions to urban development problems is unfounded. Not all state sponsored community participation programmes in the Third World are like the two case studies reviewed previously. It may also be argued that their successes have been overemphasized in the published reports from which they were taken (American Friends Service Committee, 1975; All India Housing Development Association, 1983). Nevertheless, they do show what can be done if government resources and community efforts are combined in a determined attempt to improve urban conditions.

The case studies do show also that in spite of a long standing tradition of centralization, bureaucratization and professionalization in urban development, as well as a high degree of antipathy to community participation ideals on the part of civil servants and planners, it is both possible and desirable to involve ordinary people in urban development. The pessimism which characterizes a good deal of the literature on the subject, claiming that participation ideals are unworkable, is not supported by the evidence.

Nonetheless, as was suggested earlier, it would be wrong to claim that the state's response to community participation has been unequivocally supportive and that it may be categorized as constituting a true participatory mode as defined in Chapter 1 of this book. There is little evidence to show that this is the case. State responses to community participation ideas in urban development have often been haphazard and poorly formulated, and there are substantial variations in the extent to which these ideals have been applied in different countries. They have also enjoyed greater or lesser popularity depending on the preferences of senior administrators, politicians and planners. Another important factor in their implementation is the extent to which urban projects are dependent on external funding from the international agencies and non-governmental organizations. The involvement of these organizations has often been a primary catalyst for community involvement. The generally incrementalist character of present day community participation policies in urban development is all too clear.

As shown earlier in this chapter, state responses to community participation have also been manipulative in nature. Although there was little evidence of a manipulative attitude on the part of the authorities in the two case studies, the researches of Gilbert and Ward (1984) and others in Latin America reveal that some Third World governments have been able to exploit community participation programmes for their own ends. This occurs in many different ways but one of the most common is the linking of local community activities with the ruling political party. As in the communist countries where action and political party action are inseparable, political, political élites and their supporters in the non-socialist countries of the Third World have also sought to blur the distinction between spontaneous community action and the activities of the ruling party. In these cases, community groups lose their identity and capacity for independent action.

It should be recognized, however, that community participation can fail not only because of the antipathy or subversive efforts of the state but because of problems in the community. As was seen in the two case studies, morale flagged and motivation ebbed at crucial times during the implementation of the projects and there were differences of opinion between different groups. The view that once resources ar eprovided, the urban poor will spontaneously rise and take action to improve their environment and housing conditions, needs to be qualified. Community participation, as was shown in the case studies, hinges on mobilization, training and motivation. Local skills must be harnessed to specific projects and participants need to be made aware of their importance to the project. Although wider political issues cannot be ignored, the more mundane questions of organization, leadership and motivation are equally important if community participation is to bring tangible improvements in urban conditions in the Third World.

6

Participation and social work services

JAMES MIDGLEY

The rapid increase of state involvement in social development during this century has been accompanied by a gradual consolidation of bureaucratic and technocratic specialization in each of the major social service sectors. The result is that particular areas of social development such as health, education and housing are today closely identified with particular government bureaucracies. Most developing countries have functionally specialized ministries which have primary responsibility for the formulation of policies and the implementation of government programmes in these different sectors.

In addition to the major social service ministries, many governments have established what are variously known as Ministries or Departments of Social Welfare, Public Welfare, Social Services or Social Affairs. They provide services to neglected children, the physically handicapped, young offenders, the victims of disasters, dependent elderly people and various others in need. Their programmes, which are largely remedial in orientation, are closely associated with the activities of professional social workers.

Ministries of Social Welfare, as they will be called in this chapter, are primarily an Anglophone invention having been established in the British colonies in the middle decades of this century. Mair (1944) reported that their creation owes much to the activities of the Advisory Committee on Social Welfare which, like similar committees concerned with health, education and penal matters, operated within the Colonial Office in London to assist in the formulation of colonial social development policy. Of course, the committee's activities were closely linked to overall British colonial policy which was concerned with law and order, the maintenance of favourable conditions for trade and economic exploitation and, towards the end of the colonial era, the creation of stable political institutions (Mayo, 1975). It is perhaps not surprising that some of the first colonial welfare departments were established in the British West Indies in the wake of serious civil disobedience and popular discontent. Another relevant factor was the expansion of statutory welfare in the metropolitan countries. The coming of the so-called 'welfare state' in Britain inspired some colonial policy makers and their advisers and fostered the creation of government services directed at the amelioration of conspicuous social need. There was demand also for the expansion of these services within the colonies where problems of juvenile delinquency, begging, vagrancy and destitution were becoming more acute and were being regarded by settlers and colonial administrators alike as a growing nuisance. Financial support for the provision of social work services was given through the Colonial Development and Welfare Acts which were intended to assist the colonial administrations to expand economic development programmes and to develop the social services.

In many British colonies, and particularly in Africa and the Caribbean, welfare departments were established in the 1940s and 1950s and in most cases, social workers from Britain were recruited to organize their activities. Together with the native welfare assistants as they were known in Africa, these expatriate personnel laid the foundations for subsequent developments. Local staff were sent abroad to Britain for training in social work and by the time the colonies gained independence, the departments of social welfare were firmly established. Although welfare services in some British territories such as India evolved earlier, there was a similar stress on centralized administration and professional social work intervention. Indeed, one of the first professional schools of social work in the Third World was the Tata Institute which was established in Bombay in 1936.

In the French colonies and Latin American countries, the pattern was somewhat different; here more emphasis was placed on the provision of social welfare programmes through health and social security institutes. In the Philippines, under the American colonial administration, social work services were introduced just before the First World War. Although these services were initially fragmented, they were gradually consolidated under the control of a central department as in the British territories. A similar pattern of centralized administration was adopted in countries such as Saudi Arabia and Thailand which were not colonized.

A major factor in the post-independence period was the support given to the newly formed Ministries of Social Welfare by the United Nations which played a major role in promoting professional social work and government administered social welfare services in the Third World. Various reports about juvenile delinquency, prostitution and other social problems conventionally dealt with by Ministries of Social Welfare were published and numerous conferences and expert missions to the developing countries were organized. In the 1950s and 1960s, the United Nations undertook several international surveys of social work education and together with its specialized agencies such as UNICEF, it sponsored the creation of professional social work schools in a number of developing countries. These activities gave a major boost to the expansion of the social work profession in the Third World.

Although, as pointed out earlier, Ministries of Social Welfare are known by different names in different countries, public sector organizations of this type are to be found in many developing countries today and especially in the former British territories and those with close links to the United States. Although social welfare bureaucracies are less consolidated in the Francophone and Latin American nations, there are tendencies towards the amalgamation of disparate welfare institutes and foundations and an increasing trend towards centralization. In several developing countries, social welfare services are not provided by autonomous ministries but are linked with a joint ministerial structure to departments of labour, or community development or health. But, in practice, their activities are seldom integrated and they function separately. The only exception seems to be in Africa where community development and social welfare departments often collaborate and exchange personnel. But even here the two are sometimes quite separate.

Welfare needs and state social work services

The type of service provided by Ministries of Social Welfare in the Third World reflects the conventional concerns of the social work profession and the need to respond to conspicuous and critical family and individual problems. As in the industrial countries these social problems are associated with particular social work services such as child care, probation, social assistance or family welfare. Although the range is not as extensive, the services provided by social workers in the developing countries have many similarities with those in the industrial nations.

One of these problems, which seems to have elicited the earliest forms of governmental social work intervention, is juvenile delinquency. Dubey's (1973) account of the development of social work in India revealed that provisions for young offenders were introduced by the British and that they formed the basis for subsequent developments. The first residential services were established in terms of the Reformatory Schools Act of 1876 which led through the report of the Indian Jail Committee of 1919 to the enactment of more comprehensive child care legislation in many states. Hardiman and Midgley (1982) reported that the newly established welfare departments in the African colonies usually gave priority to the introduction of social work services for young offenders. In Ghana, for example, where the first welfare officer was appointed in 1943, the department's earliest activities included the creation of a juvenile court, the recruitment of a probation officer from England and the provision of residential services for delinquent boys.

Then, as now, juvenile delinquency remains an essentially urban phenomenon. Although statistical data are limited and subject to numerous flaws and inaccuracies, Clinard and Abbott (1973) reviewed a number of research studies to show that juvenile crime is associated with urban and especially big city conditions in many developing countries. They reported also that most explanations of juvenile delinquency in the Third World emphasize the aetiological role of rapid urbanization, modernization and the disintegration of traditional forms of social control. Although this account has been disputed by Sumner (1982) whose alternative *marxisant* analysis stresses poverty, class structure, police behaviour and the ideological nature of law, young people are regularly apprehended and processed by the agents of law enforcement in societies of all ideological characteristics. The problem for the social work services which are charged with dealing with these young people is how best to provide for them.

In most developing countries services for young offenders are today much as they were when first introduced by the colonial authorities. Juvenile courts have been established within the municipal courts in many large Third World cities and usually children convicted of criminal offences are committed to residential institutions where they are taught vocational skills and subjected to rigorous discipline. Those convicted of less serious offences may be released with a caution or a fine or, in some countries where the practice is still employed, they may be sentenced to a whipping (Midgley, 1975, 1982). Although probation services have been created in many countries it appears that they are not all that widely used.

There have been few attempts to devise innovative policies for young offenders in developing countries. Clifford (1966) made a variety of proposals suggesting, for example, that probation could be modified to place young offenders under the care of traditional elders or village leaders or that alternatives to custodial reformatory care should be found. Steps could be taken also to modify the legal code to exclude various behaviours from the ambit of the criminal law. But with few exceptions, new approaches have not been adopted and services for young offenders in the Third World continue to follow the old colonial model.

Another major field of social work service in the developing countries is child care. Like services for young offenders, child care provisions were also introduced during colonial times. They were primarily directed at orphaned, abandoned or vagrant children or at those whose families were unable to care for them. As in the industrial countries, the care of these children was initially entrusted to the Church or the secular charities and many built orphanages to accommodate them. Gradually, however, the state began to regulate their activities and with the enactment of comprehensive child care legislation, it began to provide services of this kind directly.

One of the earliest examples of state involvement in child care comes from the Philippines where the American colonial administration established the Bureau of Dependent Children in 1918. Modelled on the Children's Bureau in the United States, it administered the government orphanage, supervised the children's homes of the charities and began to undertake research into infant mortality (Landa Jocano, 1980). The state governments of India were also early leaders in the field. The first child care legislation in the country was the Children's Act of Madras (1920) and similar statutes were also enacted in Bengal (1922), Bombay (1924) and the Central Provinces (1928). As noted earlier, these acts were passed in response to the report of the Indian Jail Committee. They also led to the emergence of the state welfare departments, the first of which Jagannadham (1974) reported, was established by the Nizam of Hyderabad. In most other British colonial territories, legislation of this type was introduced later and often the English Children and Young Person's Act of 1933 was used as a model for these statutes (Midgley, 1981).

MacPherson's (1982) review of the present day child care programmes of Ministries of Social Welfare in developing countries concluded that they are urban centred, minimal in coverage and scope and based on directly imported western approaches. Sometimes the services provided by voluntary organizations are more extensive than those of government but they usually take the form of residential care. In a number of countries, international charities based in Europe or North America are the primary providers of residential facilities to needy children. The consequence of this dependence on western aid has, MacPherson (1982) argued, perpetuated inappropriate child welfare strategies which rely largely on institutional care.

While many child care statutes in developing countries do make provision for foster care and adoption, these measures are seldom used and, as will be shown, they are often inappropriate to the local culture. A more widely utilized non-residential technique is the enforcement of child maintenance. This measure was introduced into many developing countries by colonial welfare policy-makers who believed that the problems of child neglect could be reduced if men who had deserted or failed to provide for their dependents were compelled to support them (Midgley, 1981).

The conventional child care activities of most Ministries of Social Welfare contrast sharply with the critical problems of malnutrition, poverty and deprivation facing the majority of the Third World's children who live with their families in the villages and urban areas of developing countries. Various studies (UNICEF, 1983; Mendelievich, 1979) have shown that in spite of considerable progress during this century, infant mortality rates are still high, many children attend school irregularly, malnutrition is endemic, large numbers of children work long and arduous hours and many live in unsatisfactory housing conditions. Although remedial child welfare services are obviously needed, the concentration of the efforts of Ministries of Social Welfare on a relatively small number of deprived children who are without family support cannot form the basis for a comprehensive child care strategy. A strategy of this kind must pay attention to the needs of the millions of impoverished, malnourished and illiterate children who are currently ignored by Ministries of Social Welfare simply because they live with their families.

The argument that existing child care policies in developng countries need to be extended to respond to the problems of children living in conditions of mass poverty and underdevelopment has gained greater acceptance in recent times. Largely through the initiative of UNICEF, some Ministries of Social Welfare are altering existing policy approaches and adopting innovative strategies in the field. Some of these involve the development of community based child care programmes and will be referred to again later in this chapter.

Since their inception, Ministries of Social Welfare have also been concerned with problems of destitution, vagrancy and begging. Indeed, since many dependent old people, needy children and the physically handicapped were engaged in begging, more specialized provisions for them often emerged from the attempts of colonial welfare departments to suppress mendicity. Midgley (1981) reported that vagrancy and mendicity in the urban areas were regarded as major nuisances by the colonial governments. The penal codes of many colonies contained prohibitions on begging and institutions known as Work Homes or Beggars' Homes were established to accommodate and ostensibly rehabilitate those apprehended by the police. Emulating the Poor Laws, many colonial governments also made provision for the compulsory repatriation of beggars to the rural areas from where they had come. In some colonies, steps were taken to establish limited social assistance schemes which would pay small means tested benefits to enable destitute people to support themselves. However, relatively few colonies established schemes of this type and in some countries, social assistance provisions were only introduced after independence.

Midgley's (1984c) study of social assistance in the Third World reviewed information for 25 countries. It revealed that the majority of these schemes covered a variety of contingencies but that some catered only for specific contingencies such as old age or disability. In India, for example, social assistance is limited to destitute physically handicapped or elderly people who have no relatives to support them. In others, such as Zimbabwe, social assistance provides short term coverage to all indigent people except those in regular employment. As in most other countries, the award of social assistance is linked to the provision of other social work services designed to encourage claimants to become self-supporting again.

Social assistance schemes in most developing countries are inadequately funded and generally provide very meagre benefits. In some cases, these schemes are virtually defunct because of a lack of resources. Many are limited in coverage often concentrating resources in urban areas. In many cases, they perpetuate anachronistic poor law principles inherited from colonial times (Midgley, 1984d). Although attempts have been made in some countries to modify social assistance principles to provide new forms of social protection to needy people (Midgley, 1984e) examples   of innovative policy-making in this field are limited.

As was suggested previously, government social work services for needy old and physically handicapped people in the Third World often evolved out of the efforts of colonial administrations to suppress begging. The elderly and disabled were conspicuous among the beggars and, in time, it was recognized that they should not be incarcerated together with the able-bodied mendicants in the Beggars' Homes or the rehabilitation centres. In some countries, old age homes were built specifically to house destitute old people while in others, the Beggars' Homes were gradually transformed into specialized institutions for the elderly.

Apart from providing residential services, few Ministries of Social Welfare have formulated coherent policies for the elderly. The belief that the numbers of old people in the population is small and that their relatives will care for them seems to have engendered an attitude of complacency. There is concern, however, that as life expectancy increases, Third World countries will experience many of the problems associated with ageing that have been encountered in the west. Furthermore, as the United Nations (1975c) observed, action is needed because the emigration of the young has resulted in increasing numbers of dependent elderly people in the rural areas of developing countries who are without adequate support.

Although residential care is also widely used to cater for the disabled, emphasis has gradually been placed on the provision of medical or orthopaedic services, education and vocational training and today many governments now rely exclusively on residential facilities. Nevertheless, vocational training is still provided largely in residential settings and because of their remoteness from the communities to which the disabled are eventually returned, these programmes have a high failure rate. It is being gradually recognized that community based schemes for the handicapped are a preferable form of intervention. This argument will be examined again later in this chapter.

Ministries of Social Welfare are also engaged in activities designed to suppress prostitution and to prevent the recruitment of young women into commercial sexual activities. In India, services of this kind were first established in the 1920s, after the Indian government became a signatory to the Geneva Convention on the Suppression of Immoral Traffic in Women and Children of 1921. Dubey (1973) observed that various states including Bombay, Madras, Uttar Pradesh and Bengal passed legislation to deal with this problem in the 1920s. As in many other countries, however, residential care has been a primary but largely ineffective response.

This is true also of social work services designed to cater for those suffering from psychiatric illnesses. Following the European practice, many colonial governments built asylums in which the mentally ill could be incarcerated. These facilities survive in many developing countries today and in spite of advances in the treatment of mental disease, they often continue to operate exclusively as custodial institutions. Social workers are often employed in these institutions but their role is limited to liaising with relatives of the inmates or with dealing with their family problems. Unlike the industrial countries where social workers are being extensively used in the treatment of mental illness in the community, very few developing countries have made much progress in the field.

Although Ministries of Social Welfare in developing countries also provide other services, those mentioned here are undoubtedly the most common and, in many cases, form the core of state social work service provisions. Although they have undoubtedly helped to deal with serious problems of conspicuous neglect, there is widespread concern that their role is far too narrowly focused on remedial activities. The United Nations Conference of Ministers Responsible for Social Welfare which was held in New York in 1968 (United Nations, 1969) to discuss their activities, hoped that wide ranging reforms would be carried out. But these hopes have not been fulfilled and generally government social work services in the developing countries continue to experience serious problems.

The problems of state social work

Several negative references have already been made to the remedial emphasis in social work services in the developing countries. It has often been argued that this emphasis is unsuited to the needs of Third World societies where the wider problems of mass poverty and underdevelopment require the mobilization of all available resources for economic growth. The allocation of scarce resources for the treatment of delinquent children or the rehabilitation of beggars would seem to be marginal to the needs of these societies. As Livingstone (1969) revealed, this is a common criticism of Ministries of Social Welfare in many parts of the Third World: politicians, senior civil servants and planners often take the view that the budgetary allocations made to the social work services are a wasteful form of consumption expenditure and many privately question the need for services of this type.

The United Nations Conference of Ministers Responsible for Social Welfare reiterated many of these criticisms and although it recognized the need for remedial intervention, it urged governments to formulate policies that would stress the preventive and developmental functions of social welfare. Unfortunately, it provided few concrete examples of what the developmental approach entailed and although it has since become fashionable in social work circles to laud the virtues of developmental strategies, few social work policy makers have a clear idea of how such strategies may be formulated; consequently, few governments have given much emphasis to developmental social work activities.

Hardiman and Midgley (1982) argued that it is not the provision of remedial services as such that should be criticized but that the remedial orientation is given disproportionate emphasis. Equally problematic, they claimed, is the fact that remedial services are largely inappropriate to the needs and circumstances of developing countries. This is exemplified by the widespread use of residential services for nearly all forms of remedial intervention and a dependence on casework methods. Indeed, the excessive emphasis on residential care is probably the most glaring example of the inappropriateness of social work services in the Third World. Although remedial forms of intervention which do not rely on residential services can be promoted, few Ministries of Social Welfare have sought to identify alternative approaches. Even where non-residential methods are used, they are often inappropriate to Third World conditions.

One example of this comes from the field of child care. Many Ministries of Social Welfare in the Third World have replicated metropolitan child care legislation, which makes provision for foster care and adoption, without realizing that both techniques are often culturally unacceptable. Adoption is unthinkable in Islamic culture and in many African societies both adoption and foster care are regarded as forms of child selling. In animist societies, families will not take in the children of strangers since they do not know if the spirits that attend the child are benevolent or malevolent. Citing the work of Nyerenda, MacPherson (1982) reported that the number of children adopted in Zambia declined sharply after the country gained independence. This was because the settlers and colonial civil servants who were the main source of infants placed for adoption as well as the main adoptive parents, had left the country.

Another problem is that most Ministries of Social Welfare have limited coverage concentrating resources on relatively small groups of deprived people usually in the urban areas of developing countries. This problem has its origin in the colonial period when the first social welfare programmes were introduced to deal with the most conspicuous problems of urban destitution, neglect and deviance. As noted previously, pressures from the European expatriate population for action against beggars, delinquents and other 'nuisances' were a major reason for the creation of the social work services. Although some progress has been made in extending these services both in terms of geographic coverage and the identification of non-remedial forms of intervention, many governments continue to confine their social work services to the cities, concentrating on the most critical manifestations of need. It is axiomatic that the formulation of more appropriate social work policies in developing countries requires the extension of welfare to the population as a whole. As MacPherson (1982) argued, the social work services must maximize welfare for the mass of the people instead of functioning primarily to minimize, at as little cost as possible, the worst manifestations of distress. This argument can be illustrated by referring to the problems of child care discussed earlier. Ministries of Social Welfare must introduce services that cater for all needy children and not only for those who are without family support.

Ministries of Social Welfare in developing countries also face serious resource problems. Although resource scarcity is a common feature of public administration in developing countries, it is particularly severe in the social welfare field. A United Nations (1979) study of public expenditures in developing countries found that in the mid-1970s, both social security and social work service programmes received less than one per cent of gross domestic product in two thirds of the developing countries for which information was available. Hardiman and Midgley (1982) cited various reports of serious resource shortages in a number of developing countries which revealed that social workers were often unable to carry out the tasks assigned to them because of a lack of support facilities. These problems were exacerbated by a shortage of funds to provide urgently needed services to clients.

In many developing countries these problems are associated with low morale among staff. Social workers are often frustrated by their conditions of service and feel that they are not respected by other professionals and civil servants from other ministries who appear to have little understanding and sympathy for their work. Many have indicated a strong desire to leave the profession to work in commerce or industry and indeed, many have done so (Midgley, 1981: Hardiman and Midgley, 1982). This general sense of malaise has resulted in a deterioration of standards of service delivery, poor management and a noticeable lack of policy innovation in many countries. Consequently, Ministries of Social Welfare are often accorded a very low status in the hierarchy of government and continue to be regarded as marginal to national development. But, as Livingstone (1969) pointed out, social workers are partly to blame for this state of affairs since they have hardly attempted to justify their philosophy and activities to politicians and planners.

Consequently, they find themselves in a vicious cycle in which their perceived lack of relevance to the needs of developing countries perpetuates low budgetary allocations, low morale and the continuation of poor standards of service and inappropriate policies.

The role of community participation

Growing criticism of state social work services since the 1960s has resulted in a gradual recognition that new approaches are needed. As was noted earlier, the Conference of Ministers Reponsible for Social Welfare urged that development strategies, which would promote the welfare of the population as a whole, be formulated. But because the developmental concept was poorly defined and could not be readily translated into operational terms, few governments have made much progress in attempting to reorientate their conventional approaches.

Community participation offers new opportunities for Ministries of Social Welfare to extend their conventional activities to contribute positively to development and to restructure existing remedial services. Of course, local communities already bear a considerable burden of caring for needy people. Indeed, it is often only when the family or the community does not respond that Ministries of Social Welfare intervene. An alternative community based strategy would link government social work services and community responses to provide a more effective means of support. It would also provide opportunities for the promotion of developmentally relevant social work services.

Social work has long experience of community work practice. As was pointed out at the beginning of this chapter, community work is one of the three primary methods of social work intervention. But with few exceptions, community work is hardly practised in the Third World. Ministries of Social Welfare have not employed community work methods to any great extent and although some religious and voluntary agencies have promoted this approach, their activities are limited. In Africa, where community development is a feature of social welfare, remedial social work and community development functions are sometimes separated and entrusted to different personnel working in distinct administrative settings. Nevertheless, community work techniques have obvious relevance to the formulation of community based forms of intervention envisaged by the proponents of developmental social work. The question is whether Ministries of Social Welfare will respond by extending community based social work services that involve the extensive participation of local people.

Before examining this question further, illustrative case studies of attempts to develop community based social work services may elucidate the arguments for a wider role for the social work services in developing countries. Although relatively little has been published on the subject, the studies selected for inclusion here provide some indication of developments in the field.

Community participation and child care

The *crèche* or *kindergarten* is a well established form of preschool child care in the industrial countries and also in the cities of the Third World, where it is used by middle-class families and especially those with working mothers. In addition to caring for children, these institutions place considerable emphasis on educational activities and are often regarded by the middle class as a means of enhancing their children's learning opportunities and preparing them for school. Although they are not always regarded as a vehicle for providing welfare services to the poor, a number of Ministries of Social Welfare in the Third World are now using preschool day care centres for this purpose.

UNICEF played a major role in the development of this approach and this reflected a gradual change in its own attitude towards child welfare policy. Recognizing the extent of malnutrition and ill health among young children in developing countries, it called on governments to establish services which would deal directly with these problems. Community based day care facilities which provide supplementary nutrition, constructive recreation and basic medical care were thought to offer an appropriate means of extending developmental child care services to the poor communities.

A well documented example of the adoption of this strategy is the Integrated Child Development Service Scheme in India, which was established on an experimental basis in 1975. The Ministry of Social Welfare had previously supported the activities of voluntary organizations operating day care centres by assisting them to provide the children with nutritious foods. The new programme developed this approach by using the day care centre or *anganwadi*, as it is known, as a focal point for various community based activities directed at young children and women. These include preschool education, supplementary nutrition, immunization, medical check-ups, referrals and functional literacy and health education for the mothers. Each centre is staffed by a trained *anganwadi* worker who is usually recruited from the local community; she is assisted by volunteer helpers most of whom are the mothers of children. The *anganwadi* workers are supervised by para-professional staff under the direction of the Child Development Project Officer who is usually a professionally qualified social worker. Each *anganwadi* has a co-ordinating committee made up of the staff and members of the community.

The first *anganwadis* were established in thirty-three development blocks throughout the country. These were especially chosen because of their low incomes and relative deprivation. Altogether, 171 *anganwadis* were opened in these blocks. On the basis of a successful evaluation by the Indian planning commission, the programme was extended and by 1982 it was operating in 300 blocks which together contained more than 20,000 *anganwadis*; studies indicate that more than a million children were being catered for in these centres (India, 1983). The scheme is presently financed entirely by the central government and administered through the states but it is hoped that eventually local voluntary organizations will assume responsibility for administration and finance (India, 1980).

Although subsequent evaluation studies by the planning commission and other independent organizations revealed that the scheme has a significant impact on the health status of young children in the project areas, its organization especially at the block level, left much to be desired. The projects were often haphazardly managed and co-ordination of the various inputs from other ministries such as health and education was poor. On the other hand, community attitudes towards the scheme were very favourable and it appears that local *anganwadis* had done much to increase awareness of the problems of child welfare. However, the studies indicated that much more was needed to be done to involve local people in the administration and management of their centres. Although local committees were well represented with women and people from the poorest sections of the community, their role was limited. In many cases, they met infrequently and in some communities, especially in deprived urban areas, no committees had been established.

The Indian scheme has brought undoubted benefits to local communities, but it is sponsored and administered by the state and in spite of its intention to promote community participation, local people have only been marginally involved. In contrast to the Indian scheme, Bashizi (1979) provided an example of the efforts of local women in Senegal to establish their own day care centres. Because women have heavy agricultural responsibilities, and young girls who previously cared for infants now go to school, the need for alternative forms of child care became pressing. Bashizi reported that fifty-eight centres catering for more than 6000 children had been established in the rural areas of the country on the initiative of the women with some support from the men who were usually involved in their construction. The government supported the activities of the women by providing immunization and basic medical services. It also provided facilities for the training of the volunteers who staff the centres. However, as Bashizi observed, the centres are very short of funds: local people are too poor to equip and maintain them properly and government support has not included direct financial aid. Most communities have also had difficulty in recruiting volunteers to run the centres since most village women have limited free time to devote to this task.

Community services for the disabled

It was suggested previously that many developing countries have made some progress in providing services that seek to rehabilitate and integrate handicapped people into the community. Vocational training is now widely used but it is still provided mainly at large centres often located near the capital city, well away from the disabled person's home. When returned to their villages, many are unable to apply their skills because of a lack of suitable materials, employment opportunities or markets. Also, as Mia (1983) pointed out with reference to Bangladesh, specialized facilities for the handicapped usually cater for only a small proportion of those in need. Since it is unlikely that developing countries can establish a network of sophisticated, orthopaedic vocational training centres to cater for all handicapped people, an alternative community based approach is needed. An advantage of this approach, he suggested, is that it can help to facilitate preventive measures. By involving local communities in the care of the disabled and increasing their awareness of the problem, they may come to appreciate that many forms of disability can be prevented through comparatively simple procedures. Various forms of community care for handicapped people in developing countries have been provided, usually on an experimental basis. One involves the delivery of services to the disabled in their own homes. Another emphasizes the need for small community based centres which provide day care services and a focal point for local activities. Another seeks to utilize existing facilities such as the schools and health centres for the delivery of services to the handicapped. It is, of course, possible to combine these different approaches.

An example of the provision of services to disabled people in their own homes comes from the Philippines where the Ministry of Social Services and Development, with the support of the Helen Keller Foundation, is operating a project of this kind. Instead of sending blind people to residential institutions, fully trained instructors visit them at home. In the early stages of the training, blind people are taught simple mobility and domestic skills. They are then assisted to develop their potential for self-employment. This may involve training in handicrafts, dressmaking, poultry farming and other productive activities that may be commercially viable in the community. Initially, the instructor visits the trainees daily but as they progress, these visits are reduced. However, their progress and ability to function independently is carefully monitored.

A similar technique was developed in Jamaica where a project funded by a Canadian foundation and the Jamaican government sought to provide domiciliary services to families with mentally handicapped children. An interesting feature of this project is its use of local women, who have little if any formal education, to visit the homes and work with the family to develop their child's potential. The women, who are known as child development aides, are carefully trained and paid a small salary. They work closely with the project's staff and after a small assessment of each child, implement a planned educational programme through weekly visits. An evaluation of the scheme revealed that children with mild or moderate handicap made significant progress. Although steps were being taken to extend the project to areas outside the capital city, Thorburn (1981) revealed that serious financial constraints were hindering progress.

Boucebci's (1981) account of day care centres for mentally handicapped children in Algeria illustrated an alternative approach. Dissatisfied with a shortage of places in the country's residential institutions for the mentally handicapped, a group of parents in 1970 established a small day care centre in the city of Algiers where their disabled children could be brought and taught various skills. Their efforts attracted widespread attention and resulted in the creation of a national association for the care of the mentally handicapped which, with government support, has now established a network of neighbourhood centres throughout the country. The activities of the association has increased public concern for the problem, and following their representations, it is now govenment policy that facilities for the disabled should be provided by ordinary *crèches* and schools.

The state and community participation in social work

As noted previously, state social work services in the Third World are highly centralized, bureaucratically administered and dependent on professional staff who are often trained in western social work theories and methods and poorly equipped for the tasks assigned to them. They are also poorly administered, badly funded and characterized by an excessive reliance on inappropriate remedial services such as residential care which cater for small groups of people in desperate need. The case studies are rare examples of attempts to develop community based services which offer the involvement of local people.

Although government social work policy makers are undoubtedly aware of the new emphasis which is being placed on community participation, few have identified ways in which community involvement may be promoted. As was suggested earlier, policy innovation is not a distinguishing feature of social work planning in developing countries. Since few Ministries of Social Welfare have formulated a policy on community participation, it is difficult to know what their attitude towards this idea might be. But there is little reason to suppose that social work administrators and policy makers would be intrinsically opposed to it. Although they will, like other civil servants, be wary of measures that threaten their interests or weaken their authority, the available evidence suggests that most would not be hostile to the idea that ordinary people should be involved in the creation and operation of local services. The case studies support this contention as does the experience of Ministries of Social Welfare in Africa and elsewhere which have sponsored community development programmes.

However, this notion of community participation is rather different to that of community participation as defined in Chapter 1. As was suggested there, the participatory mode involves local people in decision-making as well as implementation and lays emphasis on the ability of the community to establish its own projects, and to run them without external directive. The full involvement of ordinary people in decision-making is likely to pose difficulties for many social work administrators who have a firm belief in their technical expertise and professional competence. These difficulties, as well as the general administrative and organizational features of Ministries of Social Welfare, suggest that a participatory mode will not be implemented. But, at the same time, an anti-participatory mode is not likely to characterize the response of social workers. Nor, because of their general lack of authority, access to resources and marginal role in government, are Ministries of Social Welfare likely to adopt a manipulative mode. Instead, their approach is likely to be primarily incrementalist in character.

Nevertheless, state support for community participation in social welfare would be beneficial. The case studies reveal that projects which received limited financial aid from government experienced serious difficulties even though they had enthusiastic local support. They also suggest that however willing local people may be to participate, they are often too poor to fund their own programmes and many have little free time to devote to these projects. The risk that substantial state involvement will diminish community participation and weaken local initiative is a real one. But if the welfare of the poorest sections of the community is to be improved, state support will be needed. The challenge is to find ways of harmonizing state and community responses to welfare need that will generate adequate resources while at the same time maximizing local involvement.

PART III

7

Community participation, the state and social policy

JAMES MIDGLEY

This book has shown that community participation is now an important and popular issue in development studies. Drawing inspiration from a variety of philosophical and ideological antecedents, contemporary community participation concepts combine elements of western community work and Third World community development practice to articulate a set of propositions for the active involvement of ordinary people in the development process. These propositions have been formulated by officials at the international agencies with particular reference to social development since it is here that they are thought to have particular utility. Today, community participation ideals are being extensively promoted in the fields of health, education and housing. Earlier conceptions of community involvement which found application in centralized and bureaucratically administered community development programmes have been translated into a new rhetoric of community participation in social development. But unlike the old community development approach, the new concept of community participation involves an aggressive critique of existing power structures and social conditions and requires a far more direct role for ordinary people in deciding matters affecting their welfare. By involving the poor in decision-making and the implementation of programmes, it is believed that social conditions can be radically improved.

Although the literature on the subject has grown rapidly during the last fifteen to twenty years, few systematic attempts have been made to examine the relationship between the state and community initiative in social development. This is partly because many community participation theorists have rejected state involvement out of hand and have refused to consider the issues. Many are implacably opposed to the idea that the state can contribute effectively to the promotion of community participation. This, it is argued, simply perpetuates the old 'top–down' approach to social development which imposes programmes and services on a passive population. State sponsorship of community participation stifles initiative and weakens local self-reliance. State involvement also undermines community solidarity and subverts local authority. Most proponents of community participation would avoid state involvement and seek instead to strengthen the community's capacity to deal with its own problems through its own initiative and effort.

While these views are popular, they ignore the fact that the role of the state in modern society has expanded enormously during this century. The state has also substantially extended its activities in the field of social development. The state is today a major provider of social development services and, as policy maker, it largely determines how social development programmes will evolve. The state also has the power to shape and determine the nature of community participation activities in many Third World societies. To ignore the role of the state in any discussion of community participation would, therefore, appear to be a serious omission.

This book has attempted to address the question of state and community relations in social development directly. It has done so with particular reference to the major social sectors of health, education, housing, rural development and social work services. Reviewing the activities of the state in each sector, it has attempted to document the present attitudes of government towards community participation and to discover whether any progress has been made in harmonizing state and community efforts in the field. Selected case studies have been employed to illustrate the arguments.

This concluding chapter seeks to draw the material in Part II of the book together. It attempts specifically to deal with a number of issues. Firstly, it hopes to discover what present day government attitudes towards community participation are and to examine the nature of state sponsorship and support for community participation programmes. It seeks also to locate present day responses into one or more of the major 'modes' described in the concluding section of Chapter 1. On the basis of its findings, it asks whether there are effective alternatives to the involvement of the state in community participation and whether ways can be found of harmonizing state and community relations in the promotion of social development.

State responses to community participation

As was suggested in Chapter 1 of this book, it is possible to formulate a typology of likely state responses to community participation in social development. This typology suggests that the state may act in several ways when responding to community participation. It may firstly, suppress all attempts at community participation or, secondly, it may actively promote community participation seeking to mobilize the whole community for social development and to encourage maximum involvement in decision-making. The state may thirdly attempt to use community participation programmes for ulterior motives and seek to manipulate these programmes for its own ends. Finally, the state may have a vaguely formulated or poorly implemented policy on community participation; while it does not seek to suppress community participatory activities, it fails to provide adequate support. These four hypothetical responses were denoted as the anti-participatory mode, the participatory mode, the manipulative mode and the incremental mode. Of course, these are ideal-typical responses which may not fit the situation in all countries. Also, combinations or variations of these responses may occur. Nevertheless, the typology is of value in classifying and analysing the ways governments react towards community participation activities in the Third World.

The authors of the chapters in Part II of this book have paid particular attention to the state's attitude towards community participation in the major fields of social development. They have reviewed the literature and drawn on their own knowledge and experience to examine this question. Although it is not easy to reach final conclusions or to make generalizations that apply to all developing countries, they have identified general patterns and trends.

None of the authors took the view that present day government responses to community participation were anti-participatory in character. Although they recognized that some Third World governments have reacted viciously towards participatory activities, this response was untypical and there was little evidence to suggest that the majority of community participation programmes in the Third World would be stamped out with brutal determination.

But neither were the authors able to categorize state responses to community participation as falling into the participatory mode. They were unable to conclude that Third World governments are actively encouraging or supporting community participation programmes in ways that conform to the ideals of authentic participation as defined in the literature. Many governments had declared their support for community participation and in a number of cases, governments had provided finance, staff and other resources. But generally, this suport was conditional or externally imposed and it fell short of the ideals of devolution and self-determination. In spite of the rhetoric of most state supported programmes, poor communities were not fully involved in decision-making and they did not have final say over matters that affected their own welfare. Nor did these programmes always mobilize the poorest groups in the community or bring about significant changes in power or in social and economic conditions.

Although the authors of the chapters in Part II did not feel able to classify state responses as participatory in nature, they used a number of case studies that were optimistic in tone showing that ordinary people could co-operate and participate effectively in social development programmes. A number of these projects received state support and with one or two exceptions, it was felt that state support was beneficial. However it must be stressed that the case studies were not designed to test hypotheses about state involvement but rather to illustrate the arguments. Obviously, an empirical examination of this issue cannot rely on a handful of case studies. It should be remembered also that community participation projects that are written up and published are likely to be successful ones; failures are less likely to be reported. Also, reports of successful projects tend to emphasize the positive aspects of these projects. For this reason, the authors drew conclusions from their knowledge of the field and from the general literature rather than the experiences of particular projects. And, setting aside the achievements of these projects, they could find little evidence of the adoption of a participatory mode by governments in the Third World.

Community participation, the state and social policy

On the other hand, they have produced a good deal of evidence to show that state responses to community participation are incremental in character. Many Third World governments employ the rhetoric of community participation in national development plans and other official documents and many have established administrative procedures for implementing community participation principles. Many have endorsed the community participation ideals contained in the resolutions and policy statements of the international development agencies. Civil servants from the developing countries have played a very important role in the formulation of these policies and have been active as consultants and members of international gatherings where these issues are discussed. The social development policies of Third World governments increasingly reflect a new emphasis on participatory strategies and this is particularly marked in the fields of health care and housing. But, in spite of these developments, state support for community participation programmes in many developing countries has been haphazard and *ad hoc*. With few exceptions, state resource allocations to participatory projects have been inadequate and often the ideals of community participation have been lost in the administrative inefficiencies of government administration. Bureaucratic indifference, procedural delays and many other administrative problems have effectively blocked the realization of authentic forms of community participation.

In addition to identifying a prevalent tendency towards incrementalism, the authors found evidence of a manipulative attitude on the part of the state. Although this attitude was not noticeably evident in the fields of health care and social work, it was more marked in housing and urban development and in education and rural development. Here governments often use community participation programmes for ulterior motives. In the case of education, for example, government sponsored community schooling programmes are widely employed to inculcate the ideologies of ruling political parties and, through encouraging the adulation of political élites, seeks to entrench their power and privilege. Similarly, in the field of popular housing and participatory urban development, governments often support squatter movements to gain political support and to contain urban conflict. Of course, there is a danger that these arguments may offer an oversimplified account of the role of the state and that a crude conspiracy theory

149

may be accepted. Such theories have enjoyed some popularity in social science circles in recent times but they have been severely criticized. More sophisticated accounts have discarded crude interpretations of the state as a monolithic structure which serves the interests of capital or a small ruling élite, and which conspires and manipulates to entrench their position. These accounts have shown that governments act with a multiplicity of motives and do so in response to a great variety of political, economic and social pressures. In these alternative explanations, the corporatist nature of the modern state is emphasized. And it is this emphasis that provides a basis for explaining the manipulative tendencies in state responses to community participation.

Advocates of state involvement in community participation will not be encouraged by these conclusions. In spite of the optimism of official publications on the subject and the resolutions of inter-national conferences, there is little evidence to show that state support and community initiative have been effectively combined to promote authentic participation. This is not to deny that there are individual projects that have used public resources effectively and maintained a high level of community involvement in the planning, management and implementation of programmes. Also, as shown in some of the case studies included in this book, government support for community participation programmes has been beneficial. But, as the proponents of community participation point out, benefiting from a project does not mean that ordinary people have control over their own affairs. It is the effective devolution of power to local communities to decide on matters that concern their welfare and prosperity that is at the centre of the philosophy of community participation. And it is this element that is conspicuously absent from many state sponsored community participation programmes. In the light of the evidence produced in this book, the prospect of achieving authentic community participation within the framework of state supported social development programmes would seem to be remote.

Alternatives to state sponsorship

The conclusion that state sponsorship of community participation has been largely incremental and manipulative in character supports those who believe that state involvement in community participation is a contradiction in terms. They believe that whether because of bureaucratic inefficiency or a determined effort to exploit particular programmes for ulterior ends, state involvement stifles authentic community responses and defeats the ideals of genuine peoples' participation in social development. It is for this reason that many writers have a strong antipathy to the notion of state involvement in community participation programmes. Although this attitude is not always clearly articulated in the literature, it is a pervasive theme which reflects the strong populist and anarchist influences in community participation theory. Although official publications emanating from the international agencies generally advocate the integration of state and community effort in social development, many reveal a degree of scepticism about the likelihood of achieving this goal.

If state sponsorship of community participation in social development neutralizes authentic participation, what are the alternatives? One possibility is to abandon the concept of authentic participation and to accept a more limited definition which recognizes the realities of statism in modern society and the difficulties of achieving absolute popular control over local affairs and the total involvement of all members of the community. In this conception, emphasis is placed on obtaining maximum resources and services from government agencies in order to improve social conditions even if it results in a diminution of local autonomy. A second option, which will find more favour with the proponents of community participation is to do away with state involvement of any kind. Instead of sacrificing the ideals of community participation, the state is excluded and in this way, the anti-participatory tendencies inherent in state sponsorship are effectively neutralized. The rejection of all forms of state involvement is an important element in two approaches in community participation theory. One believes in spontaneity as a desirable ingredient in the participatory process while the other places faith in the role of voluntary or non-governmental organizations in the promotion of participatory activities.

As was shown in Chapter 1 of this book, some definitions of community participation emphasize the spontaneous grass-roots or 'bottom–up' elements in community participation. These occur when local people organize themselves for social development without the involvement of external agents of any kind. This type of participation is characterized by local initiative and voluntary action. Reference was made previously to a United Nations report (1981) which distinguished between spontaneous, induced and coerced participation. It pointed out that spontaneous participation came closest to the concept of authentic participation: it is an ideal form of participation which obviates the need for state involvement and thus avoids the counterparticipatory consequences of statutory sponsorship.

Although spontaneous participation may appear to be highly desirable, there are several difficulties with this idea. Some of these are conceptual revealing wider contradictory elements in the theory of community participation. For example, if spontaneous participation is so highly prized, why do the proponents of community participation continue to advocate its promotion through the use of interventionist strategies and techniques of various kinds. It is surely compatible with the ideals of spontaneous participation that local people be left to solve their own problems through their own initiative and effort. Another contradictory aspect of the advocacy of spontaneous participation is the widespread belief that ordinary people in the Third World have little potential for participation. As was shown in Chapter 1, United Nations publications have consistently argued that local communities are apathetic and indifferent and that they require the stimulus of external change agents if they are to participate meaningfully in social development. It is odd that the same organization should at the same time extol the virtues of spontaneous participation.

Another problem with the notion of spontaneous participation is the way certain forms of community organization are classed as authentic while others are not. There is a wealth of anthropological evidence to show that elaborate procedures for participation exist in rural communities throughout the Third World. But meetings of village elders or gatherings of tribal clans to discuss common problems and find solutions are seldom regarded as spontaneous participation. The exclusion of these and other forms of indigenous involvement reveals that the definition of spontaneous participation used in the literature is an externally imposed one which is based on western ideological preconceptions rather than local practices.

There are practical difficulties with the notion of spontaneous participation as well. It ignores the need for external resources which may be desperately needed by poor communities and leaves local people to fend for themsevles as best they can. For example, the belief that poor communities should establish their own health programmes and fund them from their own resources may serve the ideals of self-reliance and autonomy but it does not promote health care or the goals of social justice. It fails to recognize that local resources will be insufficient to meet local health needs and does not seek to redistribute the resources from wealthier to poorer groups.

It is doubtful also whether spontaneously organized forms of community participation are as independent of external aid as is often supposed. Even though the initiative for local social development programmes may be taken by the community, external funds and expertise is often actively sought and widely used. Midgley and Hamilton's (1978) study of community development in Sierra Leone showed that while many rural communities had organized their own projects, they made as much use as possible of public and other forms of assistance. They concluded that rural communities did not require external 'change agents' who would motivate them to engage in development activities but that they needed finance and other tangible forms of support. Similarly, the Bhoomi Sena movement in India (de Silva *et al.*, 1982), which is often cited as an ideal example of spontaneous community participation, made use of external resources of various kinds.

A second substitute for state sponsorship of community participation programmes is the use of voluntary or non-governmental oganizations. Several writers have argued that non-governmental organizations provide effective opportunities for the implementation of community participation ideals and that these organizations are more likely to promote authentic forms of participation than the state. This view has gained considerable support and many examples of successful community participation schemes in the literature are of projects that have been sponsored by voluntary rather than statutory agencies. Indeed, a number of the case studies cited in this book were initiated and supported by non-governmental organizations.

There are several reasons why the proponents of community participation advocate the involvement of non-governmental rather than statutory organizations in community participation. Unlike the state, these organizations are claimed to be dynamic, flexible and socially concerned. It is said that they are usually staffed by people who have a deep personal commitment to humanitarian and participatory ideals. They are not inhibited by bureaucratic rules and regulations and are not accountable to indifferent superiors or corrupt politicians. Nor are they constantly mindful of their career prospects and thus concerned to promote official policies rather than the interests of local people. Consequently, they identify more closely with ordinary people and are much more sensitive to local needs.

It is argued also that voluntary organizations are more effective in promoting community participation because they are innovative and adaptable. These organizations have often pioneered new approaches to social development and they can more readily test new ideas and reformulate existing approaches. Innovation and experimentation are unlikely in government organizations which are bureaucratic and resistant to change.

Voluntary organizations are also regarded by many community participation theorists as being politically progressive. It is argued that they champion radical programmes which bring about significant social change and benefits to local communities and especially the poorest groups. Unlike the state which represents the interests of élites, at both the local and national levels, voluntary organizations are more likely to identify with the oppressed and to work actively for their liberation. As Marsden and Oakley (1982) argued, radical community action is unlikely to emerge within the formal arrangements of statutory sponsorship since the state has a vested interest in maintaining the *status quo*. Public agencies are also more responsive to the pressures exerted on them by organized interest groups. Since the least organized and marginalized sections of society have little opportunity to influence government, their interests are not likely to be served by state involvement in community participation. Non-governmental organizations are not only more likely to serve the interests of the poor but they are capable of initiating schemes that increase the organizational power and consequently the political pressures that can be exerted by poor people.

Another reason for advocating the involvement of voluntary organizations in community participation is that they are able to mobilize resources for social development projects. This is particularly true of non-governmental organizations that have international links. Although it is often assumed that the voluntary sector is short of funds when compared with the state, Lissner (1977) has argued that far more financial aid for development has been mobilized through non-governmental channels than is often appreciated. Although voluntary agencies within the developing countries may not have substantial resources, it is argued that they can raise resources for projects that governments would not be willing to support.

While it is undoubtedly true that non-governmental organizations have played a major role in the promotion of community participation it cannot be claimed that their involvement has been faultless. Indeed, the use of these organizations in promoting community participation has a number of drawbacks which have not always been recognized and which may, in fact, mitigate against the emergence of authentic forms of community involvement.

Much has been made of the non-bureaucratic character of voluntary agencies and of their flexibility and adaptability. While there is much truth in this assertion, it is fallacious to conclude that bureaucratically organized management structures and the use of rules and regulations is a distinctive feature of governmental bodies. Many voluntary organizations and especially the larger one, function bureaucratically and use formal procedural rules to carry out their tasks. These elements characterize oganizations of all kinds and are not confined to public bodies only. Similarly, while flexibility and innovation have indeed typified a good deal of voluntary enterprise in the past, it cannot be argued that all non-governmental bodies are of this type. Indeed, there is evidence to show that voluntary organizations are prone to ossification particularly if they are dominated by charismatic leaders who are unresponsive to new ideas and view innovation as a threat to their authority. And it is well known that voluntary organizations are often firmly controlled by dominant personalities of this kind. The assumption that they are usually politically progressive also needs to be questioned. Many are run by middle-class individuals whose views are liberal and paternalistic rather than radically egalitarian.

In addition to questioning the idealized asumptions which have been made about voluntary organizations, it can be argued that an excessive reliance on these organizations actually impedes the realization of community participation ideals. For example, the voluntary sector suffers from a perennial problem of malcoordination and duplication of services. The leaders of these organizations are often blissfully unaware that this is happening and sometimes they are unconcerned that this form of wastage is causing problems and retarding social development. Sometimes, they compete with each other and engage in aggressive struggles to dominate a particular field of service. One example of this is the competition which has taken place in the past between voluntary organizations involved in famine relief. This has not only harmed the reputations of these organizations but has had serious repercussions for desperately needy people. A related problem is that voluntary organizations suffer from a lack of continuity. Often new programmes are launched with enormous enthusiasm but after a time this dissipates and local communities are left with unfinished projects and unfulfilled promises. These factors cause disillusionment and resentment and hinder the promotion of participatory activities.

In spite of the large volume of international aid which has been channelled to the Third World by non-governmental organizations, voluntary agencies do suffer from serious resource constraints. They are unlikely to mobilize domestic revenues on a scale that even approaches those of the state. While it is true that many poor developing countries, particularly in Africa, are becoming increasingly dependent on foreign aid provided by voluntary agencies, this dependence is hardly conducive to the promotion of self-reliance and national autonomy. Nor is a dependence on the resources provided by voluntary organizations likely to promote authentic participation. Whatever their motives and ideologies, those who control the flow of funds are likely to attach conditions to their disbursement.

A major drawback in advocating the use of non-government rather than statutory organizations in community participation is the inability of the voluntary sector to redistribute resources. Voluntary agencies may be able to allocate considerable resources to a deprived community but they are seldom able to shift resources between groups on a sizeable scale. This is not only because of the territorial localization of much voluntary effort but because these organizations have no mandatory mechanisms for transferring resources from the wealthier sections of society to fund programmes for the poorest groups. Unlike the state which has the power to mobilize and redistribute resources, voluntary agencies are dependent on charity. Another problem is that successful non-governmental organizations tend to attract more and more resources for their own projects resulting in a concentration of these resources in certain areas. Often these successful projects become showpieces and places of pilgrimage for international development tourists. While those living in the project benefit enormously and become far better off than those in the surrounding areas, the organization's programmes are not expanded or replicated to reach a wider section of the population.

Another problem with voluntary organizations is that they often reveal an unacceptable degree of arrogance in their determination to persuade local people to accept their opinions. Although their commitment is unquestioned, the leaders of these organizations usually have definite views on social development issues and this is reflected in their activities. In spite of their claims to the contrary, these predominantly middle-class people often behave as if they know what is best for the community. They are as guilty of seeking to impose their views on others as were the proponents of community development and *animation rurale*. Although old community development theories about peasant indifference and lethargy have rightly been condemned, little has so far been said about the paternalism of those who now talk about the political ignorance and apathy of the poor and advocate the use of conscientization and other methods to raise their ideological awareness. This attitude is hardly compatible with the ideals of authentic participation. Indeed, it may alienate those who hold different beliefs and mitigate against the promotion of participatory activities.

Promoting state and community relations in social development

As these arguments suggest, it is questionable whether the voluntary sector is any more able to promote authentic participation than the state. There is little evidence to show that a reliance on non-governmental organizations results magically in the emergence of genuine forms of participation. Indeed, as has been suggested, this dependence can suppress community initiative and hinder the emergence of participatory activities. The belief that spontaneous forms of participation are preferable to either state or non-governmental sponsorship may be appealing but, as has been shown, it raises difficult issues. It is certainly hard to see how a programme of action for the promotion of community participation can be based on this concept.

While these findings may be depressing, it would be wrong to conclude that nothing can be achieved through community participation. It has been argued already that participatory programmes, whether sponsored by the state or the voluntary sector, have brought tangible benefits to local people in many parts of the world. But these activities have not generally conformed to the ideals of authentic participation. Participatory programmes have not been free of state manipulation or of the imposition of external values and directions by voluntary organizations. Also, whether organized by the state or the voluntary sector, participatory programmes have experienced a great many difficulties that belie the idealism of its advocates.

These conclusions suggest that the limits of participation need to be recognized and accommodated. The idealism and rhetoric of the concept of authentic participation needs to be tempered with a realistic assessment of the possible. It is desirable also that steps be taken to deal with the paternalism and condescending attitudes contained in much community participation theory. The assumption that the proponents of community participation know what local people want and need pervades the literature. But concepts of participation that appeal to western educated middle-class activists do not always conform to the expectations of ordinary people. For many people, participation means sharing the benefits that others in society already enjoy. Why should the poor be required to construct their own schools and clinics while the wealthier sections of society have access to state provisions? By rejecting state support on the grounds that it diminishes local initiative, the proponents of authentic participation reveal a paternalism that contrasts sharply with local aspirations.

If the critical problems of mass poverty and deprivation in the Third World are to be dealt with, concerted action by the state will be needed. Local people do not have the resources to solve these problems through their own efforts alone. Nor should the poor be denied the resources made available by other groups. Participation is highly desirable but the poor cannot survive on rhetoric and idealism. While self-reliance and voluntary action should be promoted, the problems of the Third World cannot be solved at the local level. National policies and programmes that are designed specifically to eradicate poverty, starvation, endemic ill-health, exploitation and illiteracy must be formulated and implemented with all the force of concerted state intervention. Also, a more realistic and appropriate concept of community participation that seeks to enhance state and community involvement in social development is needed. This cannot be achieved through some magical formula for success but through a long term ongoing dialectical experience of bargaining, trade off and exchange. It is the art of manipulating the mechanisms of the state that should be taught rather than the rejection of state support and the avoidance of all contact with the agencies of government.

There has been some discussion in the literature about the techniques that can be adopted to realize this goal. Some of these are derived from an analysis of state–society relationships that stresses conflict and confrontational action. Others flow from a view of state–society relationships that emphasizes co-operation and consensus. In the former, local communities are taught how to deal with bureaucrats and politicians and how to approach and pressurize them. They are encouraged to have confidence in their dealings with officialdom and to refuse aid if the conditions attached to its disbursement will diminish their autonomy. A variety of confrontational techniques have been described in the literature (Hollnsteiner, 1977, 1979) and have been used effectively by different communities to resist the imposition of external decisions or to obtain access to public resources. In the consensus approach, an attempt is made to reform established civil service procedures so that consultation with local people becomes an integral part of government decision-making. Various techniques that enhance contacts between the community and the state and that increase accountability have been advocated in the literature (United Nations, 1981; Hollnsteiner, 1982b; White, 1982). These include the creation of formal mandatory procedures for consultation between officials and local communities, the introduction of training courses in participation for both civil servants and the people and the establishment of procedures for evaluating government programmes.

These proposals have been formulated by proponents of community participation who believe that it is possible to enhance state and community relations in social development. They reveal also that ways may be found of promoting more meaningful forms of community participation with a framework of organized state–community relationships. It is difficult to judge whether these proposals will be adopted or whether they will succeed in promoting better relationships between local communities and the state in social development. While the authors of this book are not sanguine about this prospect, they believe that progress can be made. The alternative is to perpetuate ideals and rhetoric without seeking to deal with the critical problems of deprivation that characterize the lives of hundreds of millions of the world's citizens.

Bibliography

Abate, A. and Teklu, T. (1982) 'Land Reform and Peasant Associations in Ethiopia: A Case Study of Two Widely Differing Regions' in A. Bhaduri and M. Rahman (Eds) pp. 58–89.

Abel-Smith, B. (1976) *Value for Money in Health Services*, London, Heinemann

Abrams, C. (1964) *Man's Struggle for Shelter in an Urbanizing World*, Cambridge, MIT Press.

Abrams, C. (1966) *Housing in the Modern World*, London, Faber & Faber.

Abrams, C., Kobe, S. and Koenigsberger, O., (1980) 'Growth and Urban Renewal in Singapore' in O. Koenigsberger *et al.* (Eds) pp. 85–127.

Adams, A. (1981) 'The Senegal River Valley' in J. Heyer *et al.* (Eds) pp. 325–53.

Ahmed, M. (1982) 'Community Participation, the Heart of Primary Health Care' in G. E. Jones and M. Rolls (Eds) pp. 255–70.

Alinsky, S. (1946) *Reveille for Radicals*, Chicago, University of Chicago Press.

Alinsky, S. (1971) *Rules for Radicals*, New York, Random House.

All India Housing Development Association (1983) *Community Participation in Shelter Projects*, New Delhi.

American Friends Service Committee (1975) *Chawama Self-Help Project, Kafue, Zambia*, Philadelphia.

Anderson, C. A. (1966) 'Literacy and Schooling on the Development Threshold' in C. A. Anderson and M. J. Bowman (Eds) pp. 347–62.

Anderson, C. A. and Bowman, M. J. (Eds) (1966) *Education and Economic Development*, London, Frank Cass.

Arole, M. and Arole, R. (1975) 'A Comprehensive Rural Health Project in Jamkhed (India)' in K. W. Newell (Ed.) pp. 70–90.

Arole, R. (1982) 'A Comprehensive Rural Health Project, Jamkhed, India' *Contact*, 10, 1–11.

Ayres, R.L. (1983) *Banking on the Poor*, Cambridge, MIT Press.

Bacchus, K. (1982) 'Integration of School and Community Learning in Developing Countries' in R. Barnard (Ed.) pp. 1–16.

161

Bagadion, B. and Korten, F. (1985) 'Developing Irrigation Organizations: A Learning Process Approach to a Participatory Program' in M. Cernea (Ed.).

Bailey, R. and Brake, M. (Eds) (1975) *Radical Social Work*, London, Edward Arnold.

Bang, A. (1983) 'Economic Self-Sufficiency in Community Health Programmes: Myth, Mirage and Nemesis' *Link*, 3, 3–6.

Barnard, R. (Ed.) (1982) *The Integration of Schools and Community Learning in Developing Countries*, London, University of London Institute of Education.

Barnett, T. (1981) 'Evaluating the Gezira Scheme: Black Box or Pandora's Box?' in J. Heyer *et al.* (Eds) pp. 306–24.

Bashizi, B. (1979) 'Day Care Centres in Senegal: A Women's Initiative' *Assignment Children*, 47/48, 165–71.

Batten, T. R. (1962) *Training for Community Development*, London, Oxford University Press.

Batten, T. R. (1965) *The Human Factor in Community Development*, London, Oxford University Press.

Batten, T. R. and Batten, M. (1967) *The Non-Directive Approach in Group and Community Work*, London, Oxford University Press.

Becker, G. S. (1964) *Human Capital: A Theoretical and Empirical Analysis*, Princeton, Princeton University Press.

Berger, P. L. (1977) *Pyramids of Sacrifice*, Harmondsworth, Penguin.

Bhaduri, A. and Rahman, M. (Eds) (1982) *Studies in Rural Participation*, New Delhi, Oxford University Press.

Bhattacharyya, S. N. (1970) *Community Development: An Analysis of the Programme in India*, Calcutta, Academic Publishers.

Blaug, M. (1972) *An Introduction to the Economics of Education*, Harmondsworth, Penguin.

Botswana (1977) *National Development Plan, 1977–1981*, Gaberone.

Boucebci, M. (1981) 'Special Education Through Neighbourhood Centres in Algeria' *Assignment Children*, 53/54, 153–63.

Bowles, S. (1980) 'Education, Class Conflict and Uneven Development' in J. Simmons (Ed.) pp. 205–31.

Brayne, F. L. (1929) *The Remaking of Village India*, London, Oxford University Press.

Breese, G. (Ed.) (1969) *The City in Newly Developing Countries*, Englewood Cliffs, Prentice-Hall.

Broady, M. (1979) *Tomorrow's Communities*, London, Bedford Square Press.

Brokensha, D. and Hodge, P. (1969) *Community Development: An Interpretation*, San Francisco, Chandler.

Bromley, R. (Ed.) (1979) *The Urban Informal Sector*, Oxford, Pergamon.

Brown, L. (1974) *In the Human Interest*, Oxford, Pergamon.

Bibliography

Bude, H. (1984) 'Primary Schools and Rural Development: The African Experience' in R. M. Garret (Ed.) pp. 200–23.

Bugnicourt, J. (1982) 'Popular Participation in Development in Africa' *Assignment Children*, 59/60, 57–77.

Burgess, R. (1979) 'Petty Commodity Housing or Dweller Control?' in R. Bromley (Ed.) pp. 1105–33.

Castells, M. (1977) *The Urban Question*, London, Edward Arnold.

Cernea, M. (1981) *Land Tenure Systems and Social Implications of Forestry Development Programs*, Washington, World Bank.

Cernea, M. (1983) *A Sociological Methodology for Community Participation in Local Investments: The Experience of Mexico's PIDER Program*, Washington, World Bank.

Cernea, M. (Ed.) (1985) *Putting People First: Sociological Variables in Development Projects*, Oxford, Oxford University Press.

Chambers, R. (1980) *Rural Poverty Unperceived: Problems and Remedies*, Washington, World Bank.

Chambers, R. (1983) *Rural Development: Putting the Last First*, London, Longman.

Chambers, R., Longhurst, R. and Pacey, A. (Eds) (1981) *Seasonal Dimensions of Rural Poverty*, London, Pinter.

Chatterjee, B. and Gokhale, S. D. (Eds) (1974) *Social Welfare: Legend and Legacy*, Bombay, Popular Prakashan.

Chenery, H., Ahluwalia, M., Bell, C., Duloy, J. and Jolly, R. (1974) *Redistribution with Growth*, London, Oxford University Press.

Clayton, E. (1983) *Agriculture, Poverty and Freedom in Developing Countries*, London, Macmillan.

Clifford, W. (1966) 'Training for Crime Control in the Context of National Development' *International Review of Criminal Policy*, 24, 1–18.

Clignet, R. (1980) 'Education and Employment after Independence' in J. Simmons (Ed.) pp. 165–78.

Clinard, M. B. (1966) *Slums and Community Development: Experiments in Self-Help*, New York, Free Press.

Clinard, M. B. and Abbott, D. J. (1973) *Crime in Developing Countries*, New York, Wiley.

Coombs, P. H. and Ahmed, M. (1974) *Attacking Rural Poverty: How Non-Formal Education Can Help*, Baltimore, Johns Hopkins University Press.

Cosio, A. (1981) 'Community Development in Mexico' in R. Dore and Z. Mars (Eds) pp. 337–432.

Coulson, A. (1981) 'Agricultural Policies in Mainland Tanzania, 1946–76' in J. Heyer *et al.* (Eds) pp. 52–89.

Colbourne, M. (1963) *Planning for Health*, London, Oxford University Press.

Craig, G., Derricourt, N. and Loney, M. (Eds) (1982) *Community Work and the State*, London, Routledge & Kegan Paul.

Cumper, G. (1972) *Survey of Social Legislation in Jamaica,* Mona, University of the West Indies Institute for Social and Economic Research.

Dag Hammarskjold Foundation (1975) *What Now? Another Development,* Uppsala.

Dahl, R. A. (1956) *A Preface to Democratic Theory,* Chicago, University of Chicago Press.

Dahl, R.A. and Tufts, E. R. (1973) *Size and Democracy,* Stanford, Stanford University Press.

Dasgupta, S. (1968) *Social Work and Social Change,* Boston, Porter Sargent.

De Kadt, E. (1982) 'Community Participation for Health: The Case of Latin America' *World Development,* 10, 573–84.

da Silva, G. V. S., Mehta, N., Rahman, M. and Wignoraja, P. (1982) 'Bhoomi Sena: A Land Army in India' in A. Bhaduri and M. Rahman (Eds) pp. 151–69.

Djukanovics, V. and Mach, E. P. (Eds) (1975) *Alternative Approaches to Meeting Basic Health Needs in Developing Countries,* Geneva, World Health Organization.

Dore, R. (1976) *The Diploma Disease,* London, Allen & Unwin.

Dore, R. and Mars, Z. (Eds) (1981) *Community Development,* London, Croom Helm.

Drakakis-Smith, D. (1981) *Urbanization, Housing and the Development Process,* London, Croom Helm.

Dubey, S. N. (1973) *Administration of Social Welfare Programmes in India,* Bombay, Somaiya.

Dwyer, D. J. (1975) *People and Housing in Third World Cities,* London, Longman.

Dyson, T. (1981) 'Preliminary Demography of 1981 Census' *Economic and Political Weekly,* 16, 1349–56.

Dyson, T. and Crook, N. (Eds) (1984) *India's Demography: Essays on the Contemporary Population,* New Delhi, South Asia Publishers.

Ecklein, J. L. and Lauffer, A. (1972) *Community Organizers and Social Planners,* New York, Wiley.

Elliott, C. (1975) *Patterns of Poverty in the Third World,* New York, Praeger.

FAO: See Food and Agricultural Organization.

Faure, E., Herrera, F., Kaddoura, A., Lopes, H., Petrovski, A., Rahnema, M. and Champion Ward, F. (1972) *Learning to Be,* Paris, UNESCO.

Flavier, J. M. (1970) *Doctor to the Barrios,* Quezon City, New Day.

Food and Agricultural Organization (1979) *Participation of the Poor in Rural Organizations,* Rome.

Foster, P. J. and Clignet, R. (1966) *The Fortunate Few: A Study of Secondary Schools and Students in the Ivory Coast,* Chicago, Northwestern University Press.

Freire, P. (1972) *Pedagogy of the Oppressed,* Harmondsworth, Penguin.

Gaikwad, V. R. (1981) 'Community Development in India' in R. Dore and Z. Mars (Eds) pp. 245–334.

Galjart, B. (1981a) 'Counterdevelopment' *Community Development Journal*, 16, 88–96.

Galjart, B. (1981b) 'Participatory Development Projects' *Sociologia Ruralis*, 21, 142–59.

Garforth, C. (1982) 'Reaching the Rural Poor: A Review of Extension Strategies and Methods' in G. E. Jones and M. Rolls (Eds) pp. 43–70.

Garrett, R. M. (Ed.) (1984) *Education and Development*, London, Croom Helm.

Gilbert, A. and Gugler, J. (1982) *Cities, Poverty and Development*, Oxford, Oxford University Press.

Gilbert, A. and Ward, P. (1984) 'Community Action by the Urban Poor: Democratic Involvement, Community Self-Help or a Means of Social Control?' *World Development*, 12, 8.

Gish, O. (1970) 'Health Planning in Developing Countries' *Journal of Development Studies*, 6, 67–84.

Gish, O. (1977) *Guidelines for Health Planners*, London, Trimed.

Gow, D. G. and VanSant, J. (1983) 'Beyond the Rhetoric of Rural Development Paricipation: How Can it be Done?' *World Development*, 11, 427–46.

Gran, G. (1983) *Development by People*, New York, Praeger.

Grant, J. P. (1983) 'A Child Survival and Development Revolution' *Assignment Children*, 61/62, 20–31.

Griffin, K. (1974) *The Political Economy of Agrarian Change*, London, Macmillan.

Hakim, P. (1982) 'Lessons from Grassroots Development Experience in Latin America and the Caribbean' *Assignment Children*, 59/60, 137–41.

Hall, A. (1978) *Drought and Irrigation in North-East Brazil*, Cambridge, Cambridge University Press.

Hall, A. (forthcoming) 'Sociologists in Foreign Aid: Rhetoric and Reality' in A. Hall and J. Midgley (Eds).

Hall, A. and Midgley, J. (Eds) (forthcoming) *Development Policy: Sociological Perspectives*, Manchester, Manchester University Press.

Haque, W., Niranjan, M., Rahman, A. and Wignaraja, P. (1977) 'Towards a Theory of Rural Development' *Development Dialogue*, 2, 1–22.

Harbison, F. H. (1973) *Human Resources as the Wealth of Nations*, Oxford, Oxford University Press.

Hardiman, M. (1984) 'Some Lessons to be Learnt from Small-scale Community Health Projects in India' in T. Dyson and N. Crook (Eds) pp. 127–40.

Hardiman, M. and Midgley, J. (1981) 'Training Social Planners for Social Development' *International Social Work*, 23, 1–14.

Hardiman, M. and Midgley, J. (1982) *The Social Dimensions of Development,* Chichester, Wiley.

Hardjono, J. (1983) 'Rural Development in Indonesia: The Top–down Approach' in D. Lea and D. Chaudhri (Eds) pp. 38–65.

Harper, E. and Dunham, A. (Eds) (1959) *Community Organization in Action,* New York, Association Press.

Hawes, H. (1979) *Curriculum and Reality in African Primary Schools,* London, Longman.

Hendriks, G. (1964) *Community Organization,* The Hague, Ministry for Social Work.

Hetzel, B. S. (Ed.) (1978) *Basic Health Care in Developing Countries,* Oxford, Oxford University Press.

Heyer, J., Roberts, P. and Williams, G. (Eds) (1981) *Rural Development In Tropical Africa,* London, Macmillan.

Hollnsteiner, M. R. (1977) 'People Power: Community Participation in the Planning of Human Settlements' *Assignment Children,* 43, 11–47.

Hollnsteiner, M. R. (1979) 'Mobilizing the Rural Poor Through Community Organization' *Philippine Studies,* 27, 387–416.

Hollnsteiner, M. R. (1982a) 'The Participatory Imperative in Primary Health Care' *Assignment Children,* 59/60, 35–56.

Hollnsteiner, M. R. (1982b) 'Government Strategies for Urban Areas and Community Participation' *Assignment Children,* 57/58, 43–64.

Horn, J. W. (1971) *Away with all Pests,* New York, Monthly Review Press.

ICSSR/ICMR: See Indian Council of Social Science Research and Indian Council of Medical Research.

IFAD: See International Fund for Agricultural Development.

India (1946) *Report of the Health Survey and Development Committee,* New Delhi.

India (1980) *Integrated Child Development Service Scheme,* New Delhi, Ministry of Social Welfare.

India (1981) *Report of the Working Group on Health for All by 2000 AD,* New Delhi, Ministry of Health and Family Welfare.

India (1983) *Report, 1982–3,* New Delhi, Ministry of Social Welfare.

Indian Council of Social Science Research and Indian Council of Medical Research (1981) *Health for All: An Alternative Strategy,* Pune.

Intermediate Technology Development Group (1971) *Health, Manpower and the Medical Auxiliary,* London.

International Fund for Agricultural Development (1983) *The Role of Rural Credit Projects in Reaching the Poor: IFAD's Experience,* Rome.

International Labour Office (1977) *The Basic Needs Approach to Development,* Geneva.

Ionescu, G. and Gellner, E. (Eds) (1969) *Populism: Its Meanings and National Characteristics,* New York, Macmillan.

Bibliography

ITDG: See Intermediate Technology Development Group.

Jagannadham, V. (1974) 'Changing Patterns in Social Welfare Administration' in B. Chatterjee and S. D. Gokhale (Eds) pp. 85–91.

John, P. C. (1982) 'The Health Care System in India: An Alternative Strategy' *Link*, 2, 1–3.

Jones, G. E. and Rolls, M. (Eds) (1982) *Extension and Relative Advantage in Rural Development*, Chichester, Wiley.

Jones, J. F. and Pandey, R. F. (Eds) (1981) *Social Development*, New York, St Martin's Press.

Karkal, M. (1982) 'Health for All: A Review and Critique of Two Reports' *Economic and Political Weekly*, 17, 249–53.

King, A. D. (1976) *Colonial Urban Development*, London, Routledge & Kegan Paul.

King, M. (Ed.) (1966) *Medical Care in Developing Countries*, Nairobi, Oxford University Press.

King, M. (1970) *Team Work for World Health*, London, Churchill.

Kitching, G. (1982) *Development and Underdevelopment in Historical Perspective*, London, Methuen.

Koenigsberger, O. (1952) 'New Towns in India' *Town Planning Review*, 23, 95–132.

Koenigsberger, O., Groak, S. and Bernstein, B. (Eds) (1980) *The Work of Charles Abrams: Housing and Urban Renewal in the USA and the Third World*, Oxford, Pergamon.

Krauhaar, R. and Schmidt de Torres, B. (1982) 'The Transformation of Community Work in the United States' in G. Craig *et al.* (Eds) pp. 143–52.

Landa Jocano, F. (1980) *Social Work in the Philippines*, Manila, New Day.

Lane, R. P. (1939) 'Reports of Groups Studying Community Organization Process' *Proceedings of the 66th National Conference of Social Work*, New York, National Association of Social Workers.

Lane, R.P. (1940) 'The Field of Community Organization' *Proceedings of the 67th National Conference of Social Work*, New York, National Association of Social Workers.

Latin American Report (1975) cited in A. Mabogunje *et al.* (1978).

Lea, D. and Chaudhri, D. (Eds) (1983) *Rural Development and the State*, London, Methuen.

Lele, U. (1975) *The Design of Rural Development*, Baltimore, Johns Hopkins University Press.

Lerner, D. (1967) 'Comparative Analysis of Processes of Modernization' in H. Miner (Ed.) pp. 21–38.

Lewis, O. (1966) 'The Culture of Poverty' *Scientific American*, 214, 19–25.

Lewis, W. A. (1955) *The Theory of Economic Growth*, London, Allen & Unwin.

Lipton, M. (1977) *Why Poor People Stay Poor*, London, Temple Smith.

Link, 2, 1–10.

Lissner, J. (1977) *The Politics of Altruism*, Geneva, Lutheran World Federation.

Little, K. (1972) *Urbanization as a Social Process*, London, Routledge & Kegan Paul.

Livingstone, A. (1969) *Social Policy in Developing Countries*, London, Routledge & Kegan Paul.

Lloyd, P. (1979) *Slums of Hope?*, Harmondsworth, Penguin.

Loney, M. (1983) *Community Against Government*, London, Heinemann,

Lucas, J. R. (1976) *Democracy and Participation*, Harmondsworth, Penguin.

Mabogunje, A., Hardoy, J. and Misra, R. (1978) *Shelter Provision in Developing Countries*, Chichester, Wiley.

MacPherson, S. (1982) *Social Policy in the Third World*, Brighton, Wheatsheaf.

Mair, L. (1944) *Welfare in the British Colonies*, London, Royal Institute of International Affairs.

Majeres, J. (1977) *Popular Participation in Planning and Decision Making for Basic Needs Fulfilment*, Geneva, International Labour Office.

Malcolm, L. A. (1978) 'The Health Care System' in B. S. Hetzel (Ed.) pp. 38–62.

Mangin, W. (1967) 'Latin American Squatter Settlements: A Problem and a Solution' *Latin American Research Review*, 2, 65–98.

Mangin, W. (1970) *Peasants in Cities*, New York, Houghton Mifflin.

Marsden, D. and Oakley, P. (1982) 'Radical Community Development in the Third World' in G. Craig *et al.* (Eds) pp. 153–63.

Martin, C. (1982) 'Basic Needs Education: Who Needs It?' *Reading Rural Development Communications Bulletin*, 15, 3–6.

Mata, L. (1983) 'The Evolution of Diarrhoeal Diseases and Malnutrition in Costa Rica: The Role of Interventions' *Assignment Children*, 61/62, 195–224.

Mayo, M. (1975) 'Community Development: A Radical Alternative?' in R. Bailey and M. Brake (Eds) pp. 129–43.

Mendelievich, E. (Ed.) (1979) *Children at Work*, Geneva, International Labour Office.

Mesa-Lago, C. (1978) *Social Security in Latin America*, Pittsburgh, University of Pittsburgh Press.

Mia, A. (1983) 'Community Participation: The Needed Approach to Primary and Secondary Prevention of Disability and Rehabilitation of the Disabled in Rural Communities' *International Social Work*, 26, 26–34.

Midgley, J. (1975) *Children on Trial: A Study of Juvenile Justice*, Cape Town, National Institute for Crime Prevention and the Rehabilitation of Offenders.

Midgley, J. (1981) *Professional Imperialism: Social Work in the Third World*, London, Heinemann.

Bibliography

Midgley, J. (1982) 'Corporal Punishment and Penal Policy' *Journal of Criminal Law and Criminology*, 73, 388–403.

Midgley, J. (1984a) 'Diffusion and the Development of Social Policy: Evidence from the Third World' *Journal of Social Policy*, 13, 167–84.

Midgley, J. (1984b) 'Fields of Practice and Professional Roles for Social Planners: An Overview' in J. Midgley and D. Paichaud (Eds) pp. 10–33.

Midgley, J. (1984c) *Social Security, Inequality and the Third World*, Chichester, Wiley.

Midgley, J. (1984d) 'Poor Law Principles and Social Assistance in the Third World: A Study of the Perpetuation of Colonial Welfare' *International Social Work*, 27, 2–12.

Midgley, J. (1984e) 'Social Assistance: An Alternative Form of Social Protection in Developing Countries' *International Social Security Review*, 84, 247–64.

Midgley, J. and Hamilton D. (1978) 'Local Initiative and the Role of Government in Community Development: Policy Implications of a Study in Sierra Leone' *International Social Work*, 21, 1–11.

Midgley, J. and Piachaud, D. (Eds) (1984) *The Fields and Methods of Social Planning*, London, Heinemann.

Miner, H. (Ed.) (1967) *The City in Africa*, London, Pall Mall.

Morley, D. (1973) *Paediatric Priorities in the Developing World*, London, Butterworth.

Morley, D. and Woodland, M. (1979) *See How they Grow*, London, Macmillan.

Morris, R. (Ed.) (1964) *Centrally Planned Change*, New York, National Association of Social Workers.

Moser, C. (1979) 'Informal Sector or Petty Commodity Production: Dualism or Dependence in Urban Development' in R. Bromley (Ed.) pp. 1041–64.

Mould, P. S. (1966) 'Rural Improvement Through Communal Labour in the Bombali District of Sierra Leone' *Journal of Administration Overseas*, 5, 29–46.

Mushi, S. S. (1981) 'Community Development in Tanzania' in R. Dore and Z. Mars (Eds) pp. 139–242.

National Council for Social Service (1960) *Community Organization: An Introduction*, London.

Newell, K. W. (Ed.) (1975) *Health by the People*, Geneva, World Health Organization.

Noor, A. (1981) *Education and Basic Human Needs*, Washington, World Bank.

Norman, D. W. (1978) *The Farming Systems Approach: Relevancy for the Small Farmer*, Ann Arbor, Michigan State University, mimeo.

Nyerere, J. K. (1967) *Education for Self-Reliance*, Dar-es-Salaam, Government Printer.

Oakley, P. and Marsden, D. (1984) *Approaches to Participation in Rural Development*, Geneva, International Labour Office.

Oakley, P. and Winder, D. (1981) *The Concept and Practice of Rural Social Development*, Manchester, Manchester Papers on Development, Studies in Rural Development, University of Manchester.

Omer, S. (1981) 'Institution Building' in J. F. Jones and R. S. Pandey (Eds) pp. 95–107.

Payne, G. K. (Ed.) (1984) *Low Income Housing in the Developing World*, Chichester, Wiley.

Pearse, A. (1980) *Seeds of Plenty, Seeds of Want*, Oxford, Clarendon Press.

Pearse, A. and Stiefel, M. (1979) *Inquiry into Participation: A Research Approach*, Geneva, United Nations Research Institute for Social Development.

Pearse, A. and Stiefel, M. (1981) *Debater Comments on 'Inquiry into Participation: A Research Approach'*, Geneva, United Nations Research Institute for Social Development.

Pennock, J. R. (1979) *Democratic Political Theory*, Princeton, Princeton University Press.

Perlman, R. and Gurin, A. (1972) *Community Organization and Social Planning*, New York, Wiley.

Portes, A. (1971) 'The Urban Slum in Chile' *Land Economics*, 47, 235–48.

Quijano, A. (1974) 'The Marginal Pole of the Economy and the Marginalized Labour Force' *Economy and Society*, 3, 393–428.

Rahman, M. (1981) *Some Dimensions of People's Participation in the Bhoomi Sena Movement*, Geneva, United Nations Research Institute for Social Development.

Rifkin, S. (1983) 'Planners' Approaches to Community Participation in Health Programmes: Theory and Reality' *Contact*, 75, 3–16.

Roberts, B. (1978) *Cities of Peasants*, London, Edward Arnold.

Roling, N. (1982) 'Alternative Approaches to Extension' in G. E. Jones and M. Rolls (Eds) pp. 87–115.

Rondinelli, D. A. (1983) *Development Projects as Policy Experiments*, London, Methuen.

Rosenstein-Rodan, P. (1943) 'Problems of Industrialization of Southern and Eastern Europe' *Economic Journal*, 53, 205–11.

Ross, D. (1979) 'The Village Health Committee: A Case Study of Community Participation in Sierra Leone' *Contact*, 49, 1–9.

Ross, M. G. (1955) *Community Organization: Theory and Principles*, New York, Harper.

Ross, M. G. (1958) *Case Histories in Community Organization*, New York, Harper.

Rostow, W. W. (1960) *The Stages of Economic Growth: A Non-Communist Manifesto*, Cambridge, Cambridge University Press.

Safa, H. I. (1974) *The Urban Poor of Puerto Rico*, New York, Holt, Reinhart and Winston.

Schumpeter, J. (1942) *Capitalism, Socialism and Democracy*, London, Allen & Unwin.

Schultz, T. (1964) *Transforming Traditional Agriculture*, New Haven, Yale University Press.

Sen-Gupta, B. (1983) 'Self-Sufficiency of Community Health Programs: Rhetoric or Reality?' *Link*, 3, 7–12.

Shah, K. (1984) 'People's Participation in Housing Action: Meaning, Scope and Strategy' in G. K. Payne (Ed.) pp. 199–208.

Shah, P. M. (1976) 'Community Participation in Nutrition: The Kasa Project in India' *Assignment Children*, 35, 53–71.

Shah, P. M. (1977) *The Kasa MCHN Project: Integrated Child Health Nutrition Model, Third Progress Report*, Bombay, Government of Maharashtra and CARE.

Shah, P. M. (1981) 'Maternal Nutrition in Deprived Populations' *Assignment Children*, 55/56, 41–72.

Shils, E. (1960) 'The Intellectuals in the Political Development of the New States' *World Politics*, 12, 329–368.

Sidel, V. W. and Sidel, R. (1975) 'The Health Care Delivery System of the People's Republic of China' in K. Newell (Ed.) pp. 1–12.

Simmons, A. B. (1978) *Slowing Metropolitan City Growth in Asia: A Review of Policies, Programmes and Results*, Paper presented to the ECLA/CELADE Seminar on Population Distribution, cited in A. Gilbert and J. Gugler (1982).

Simmons, J. (Ed.) (1980) *The Educational Dilemma: Policy Issues for Developing Countries in the 1980s*, Oxford, Pergamon.

Smith, K. H. (1982) 'International Seminar on Popular Participation, Ljubljana, May, 1982' *Assignment Children*, 59/60, 165–68.

Stewart, A. (1969) 'The Social Roots' in G. Ionescu and E. Gellner (Eds) pp. 180–96.

Stiefel, M. and Pearse, A. (1982) 'UNRISD's Popular Participation Programme' *Assignment Children*, 59/60, 145–59.

Streeten, P., Burki, S., Ul Haq, M., Hicks, N. and Stewart, F. (1981) *First Things First: Meeting Basic Needs in Developing Countries*, Oxford, Oxford University Press.

Swan, P. J. (1980) *The Practice of People's Participation: Seven Asian Experiences in Housing the Poor*, Bangkok, Asian Institute of Technology.

Sumner, C. (1982) 'Crime, Justice and Underdevelopment: Beyond Modernization Theory' in C. Sumner (Ed.) pp. 1–39.

Sumner, C. (Ed.) (1982) *Crime, Justice and Underdevelopment*, London, Heinemann.

Thomas, D. N. (1983) *The Making of Community Work*, London, Allen & Unwin.

Thompson, A. R. (1981) *Education and Development in Africa*, London, Macmillan.

Thorburn, M. J. (1981) 'In Jamaica, Community Aides for Disabled Preschool Children' *Assignment Children*, 53/54, 117–34.

Titmuss, R. M. (1964) *The Health Services of Tanganyika*, London, Pitman.

Todaro, M. P. (1977) *Economics for a Developing World*, London, Longman.

Turner, J. F. C. (1967) 'Barriers and Channels for Housing Development in Modernizing Countries' *Journal of the American Institute of Planners*, 33, 167–81.

Turner, J. F. C. (1968) 'Housing Priorities, Settlement Patterns and Urban Development in Modernizing Countries' *Journal of the American Institute of Planners*, 34, 167–81.

Turner, J. F. C. (1969) 'Uncontrolled Urban Settlements: Problems and Policies' in G. Breese (Ed.) pp. 507–30.

Turner, J. F. C. (1976) *Housing by People*, London, Marion Boyars.

Turner, J. F. C. (1980) 'What to do About Housing: Its Part in Another Development' in O. Koenigsberger *et al.* (Eds) pp. 203–11.

Unger, J. (1980) 'Severing the Links Between Education and Careers: The Sobering Experience of China's Urban Schools, 1968–76' *IDS Bulletin*, 11, 49–54.

UNICEF: See United Nations Children's Fund.

United Kingdom (1962) *Community Development: The British Contribution*, London.

United Nations (1961) *Community Development in Urban Areas*, New York.

United Nations (1962) *Report of the Ad Hoc Group of Experts on Housing and Urban Development*, New York.

United Nations (1964) *Manual on Self-Help Housing*, New York.

United Nations (1969) *Proceedings of the International Conference of Ministers Responsible for Social Welfare*, New York.

United Nations (1971a) 'Evolution of the United Nations Approach to Planning for United Socio-Economic Development' *International Social Development Review*, 3, 1–15.

United Nations (1971b) 'Highlights of the Symposium on Social Policy and Planning' *International Social Development Review*, 3, 16–31.

United Nations (1971c) *Popular Participation in Development: Emerging Trends in Community Development*, New York.

United Nations (1974) *World Housing Survey*, New York.

United Nations (1975a) *Popular Participation in Decision Making for Development*, New York.

United Nations (1975b) *Popular Participation for the Improvement of the Human Environment in Marginal Settlements*, New York.

United Nations (1975c) *The Aging: Trends and Policies*, New York.

United Nations (1976a) *Community Programmes for Low Income Populations in Developing Countries*, New York.

United Nations (1976b) *Housing Policy Guidelines for Developing Countries*, New York.

United Nations (1976c) *Report of the World Conference of the International Women's Year*, New York.

United Nations (1976d) *Report on Habitat: United Nations Conference on Human Settlements*, New York.

United Nations (1979) *Patterns of Government Expenditure on Social Services*, New York.

United Nations (1981) *Popular Participation as a Strategy for Promoting Community Level Action and National Development*, New York.

United Nations (1984) *Demographic Yearbook, 1982*, New York.

United Nations Children's Fund (1978) *Assignment Children*, 44, 1–136.

United Nations Children's Fund (1982) 'Popular Participation in Basic Services' *Assignment Children*, 59/60, 121–32.

United Nations Children's Fund (1983) *The State of the World's Children, 1984*, New York, Oxford University Press.

United Nations Research Institute for Social Development (1970) *Contents and Measurement of Socio-Economic Development*, Geneva.

United Nations Research Institute for Social Development (1975) *Rural Cooperatives as Agents for Change*, Geneva.

United Nations Research Institute for Social Development (1980) *The Quest for a Unified Approach to Development*, Geneva.

UNRISD: See United Nations Research Institute for Social Development.

Warren, R. L. (1955) *Studying Your Community*, New York, Russell Sage.

Werner, D. (1977) *Where there is no Doctor*, Palo Alto, Hesperian Foundation.

White, A. T. (1982) 'Why Community Participation?' *Assignment Children*, 59/60, 17–34.

WHO: See World Health Organization.

Wiles, P. (1969) 'A Syndrome, Not a Doctrine' in G. Ionescu and E. Gellner (Eds) pp. 166–79.

Williams, D. (1984) 'The Role of International Agencies: The World Bank' in G. K. Payne (Ed.) pp. 173–85.

Wirth, L. (1938) 'Urbanism as a Way of Life' *American Journal of Sociology*, 44, 1–24.

Wolfe, M. (1982) 'Participation in Economic Development: A Conceptual Framework' *Assignment Children*, 59/60, 79–109.

World Bank (1972) *Urbanization: Sector Policy Paper*, Washington.

World Bank (1974) *Education: Sector Working Paper*, Washington.

World Bank (1975a) *Housing: Sector Policy Paper*, Washington.

World Bank (1975b) *The Assault on World Poverty*, Baltimore, Johns Hopkins University Press.

World Bank (1980a) *Shelter*, Washington.

World Bank (1980b) *Education: Sector Policy Paper*, Washington.

World Bank (1982) *World Development Report, 1982*, Washington.

World Bank (1983) *World Development Report, 1983*, Washington.

World Health Organization (1982) *Activities of the World Health Organization in Promoting Community Involvement for Health Development*, Geneva.

Worsley, P. (1967) *The Third World*, London, Weidenfeld & Nicolson.

Worsley, P. (1969) 'The Concept of Populism' in G. Ionescu and E. Gellner (Eds) pp. 212–250.

Yeh, S. H. K. (Ed.) (1975) *Public Housing in Singapore*, Singapore, Singapore University Press.

Young, A. F. and Ashton, E. T. (1956) *British Social Work in the Nineteenth Century*, London, Routledge & Kegan Paul.

Zambia (1980) *Health by the People: Proposals for Achieving Health for All in Zambia*, Lusaka, Ministry of Health.

Name index

Subject index